BASE 66

BASE 66

◆

A Story of Fear, Fun, and Freefall

Jevto Dedijer

Translated from Swedish by
Ingrid Lang
Edited by Karl Loeffler
Cover design by Sébastien Bédard

iUniverse, Inc.
New York Lincoln Shanghai

BASE 66
A Story of Fear, Fun, and Freefall

iUniverse, Inc.

For information address:
iUniverse, Inc.
2021 Pine Lake Road, Suite 100
Lincoln, NE 68512
www.iuniverse.com

ISBN: 0-595-33510-1

Printed in the United States of America

My wonderful Cloudia. Many thanks for saving my life time and time again. I didn't always treat you well, but you never failed me, no matter what.

This book is dedicated to you.

BASE
(Building, Antenna, Span, Earth)

Requirements for membership in the exclusive BASE club include parachuting from the top of a building, an antenna tower, a bridge, and a cliff and surviving to tell the story.

*"A PERFECTLY NORMAL PERSON
IS RARE IN OUR CIVILIZATION."*
—**Karin Horney (1885-1952), Psychoanalyst**

*"IT IS GOOD TO DIE BEFORE ONE HAS
DONE ANYTHING DESERVING DEATH."*
—**Anaxandides, 250 BC, Spartan Ruler.**

Contents

Prologue

The Associated Press news release dated 7 July, 1999, immediately caught my attention: "Norwegian Daredevil Dies in Jump." Reading the short article, I gathered that a young Norwegian BASE jumper had been killed in a jump from the 3,300-foot cliff Kjeraag near Stavanger. He was a veteran jumper with more than 200 jumps from buildings, cliffs, bridges, and antennas. Despite his extensive experience, he took a huge risk by jumping in thick fog, hitting the rock wall after his canopy had opened.

My thoughts turned to my own jump from the 2000-foot cliff Trollveggen in Norway 15 years earlier. I remembered seeing my friend Bernard jump enthusiastically from the gray, bare mountain wall, heading straight for the cliff as he disappeared from view. I was overwhelmed by the shock, the lonely and incomprehensible feeling of having lost a friend. I decided to go through with the jump in Bernard's honor. I stepped up to the exit point, secured my parachute, adjusted my goggles and filled my lungs with cold fresh air. A few seconds later I was freefalling almost 2000 feet above the ground.

The Grand Old Man of Skåne

A few months after my father turned 69, he announced to my mother, my younger brother Miki and me, that he planned to take up skydiving. Of course, at first we were sure he was joking. When we realized he was serious, all three of us became quiet. He told us he had signed up for the next beginners' course held by the skydiving club Skydive Skåne. A medical statement from a doctor, approved by the Swedish Parachute Association, is needed to skydive in Sweden. Dad was certainly in good physical shape, but I still doubted he would be able to obtain the necessary statement.

My mother could only sigh when she heard about her husband Stevan's plan. This was not the first extreme idea he had come up with during their 20-year marriage. I remember my mother asking him, "Stevan, do you really need to begin skydiving at your age? You could break every bone in your body if you land too hard!"

I know my father well, and I also know that the more people doubt his ability to do something, the more decisive and stubborn he becomes. As a paratrooper in the 101st Airborne Division of the U.S. Army during World War II, he made eight jumps over Holland and Belgium. He was also a bodyguard for Maxwell Taylor, the division's general, and stayed close to him 24 hours a day. One of his jumps took place over Arnhem in Holland, not far from where part of the 101st Division was surrounded by Germans in the town of Bastogne. General Taylor was back in the States at the time, recovering from a shrapnel wound to his behind. When the Germans suggested the division surrender, the acting commander, General McAuliffe, replied, "Nuts!"

The paratroopers' chutes were made of white silk. They jumped from 1,300 feet with 65-pound packs hanging from a rope about 15 feet below. The soldiers had been taught that if the main chute did not open, they were to pull a special handle to deploy the reserve chute. Dad witnessed the deaths of many of his friends before they even had a chance to jump when the German anti-aircraft guns shot down several of the division's DC-3s. Some of the men who actually managed to jump became victims of the German sharpshooters on the ground. I'm sure that with the exception of the strong camaraderie amongst the members of the 101st Division, Dad did not have many pleasant memories of his eight wartime jumps.

My father began his physical training one month before the course was to begin. His body was a little stiff, so he concentrated on flexibility training. In the mornings, he jogged around the neighborhood, following up with knee bends, push-ups, and stretching. Every other day he ran three to four miles in fast pace. I could tell he was very nervous when the time for his check-up approached. Everything depended on the doctor's attitude toward this unusual, stubborn 69-year-old.

One day when I came home from school I found a paper taped to the mirror in the hall. In the bottom right corner were a few lines, underlined in red:

> "Stevan Dedijer is, despite his relatively advanced age, in excellent physical condition. I can not find any mental or physical reason that would prevent Stevan from skydiving."

The doctor's signature and stamp appeared on the bottom of the document. Dad had passed the first test. Proudly, he showed the medical statement to my mother when she arrived home in the evening, but she didn't exactly share his enthusiasm. The doctor was the only person who could have stopped his crazy plans. I remember bragging to my classmates that my Dad was about to go skydiving. They were all very impressed.

The course was to be spread over two weekends, with the first jump scheduled for the second Sunday. The week before the course began, Dad received an informational booklet from the skydiving club, in which he discovered that he was the same age as his three fellow students—combined. Three people were registered for the course besides my father, one woman and two men. The training started Saturday morning. They were told that students are always anxious before their first jump (big news!). The instructor explained that this was only natural, since human nature goes against jumping from flying objects 2000 feet above ground. He emphasized that they should accept their fear and at the same time try to overcome it. "The worst thing you can do is deny your fear when in reality you are terrified," he said. "This is not a sport for macho men who believe in bottling up their emotions," he concluded.

After a short introduction, the training began, switching back and forth between theory and hands-on practice. Emphasis was on emergency procedures and landings. The parachutes used in training were called TU-35s. They had been purchased from the U.S. Army in the early Sixties and were named after the shape of the air vents, which resembled the letters TU. The canopies were made of green nylon and had a surface of 1000 square feet. Together with the reserve chute, which was fastened on the abdomen, the equipment weighed about 50 pounds. Both the main chute and the reserve chute were round. A round parachute breaks the jumper's fall toward the ground; with a correctly executed PLF (Parachute Landing Fall) the jumper normally lands without injuries.[1] One hundred-fifty feet above ground, the jumper assumes the landing position: legs held together, toes up, chin against the chest, and eyes toward the horizon. The tuck-and-roll of a well executed PLF helps distribute the force of landing as evenly as possible.

The skydiving club used a swing for practicing PLFs. This contraption consisted of a metal ring fastened to a rope hanging from a stand. The student gripped the ring with both hands and the instructor put it into motion to simulate the wind factor. On the instructor's command, the student let go of the ring and executed the PLF in the sand below. This part of the training turned out to be the most difficult for Dad. He was not flexible and pliable enough in his movements when rolling in the sand. The instructor, Skuris (Scrub), provided him with some extra training in the swing. Skuris got his nickname from the resemblance of his black buzz-cut hair to a scrub brush. The first weekend of training ended with exit practice from a replica of the airplane from which they were to make their first jump. Skuris gave exit commands in quick succession:

"Ready!" Sit down in the doorway and swing legs out.

"Set!" Prepare to jump. Head high, remember the arch!

"Go!" Step off to the side, arch, and spread arms and legs.

The body position is an important part of the jump. Jumps should be performed with the chest against the propeller wind and with a solid arch to avoid ending up in an unstable position in freefall.

Dad spent the week before the jump on our front lawn, practicing landings several hours a day. Our neighbors must have wondered if he had gone completely insane: a 69-year-old man dressed in a sweat suit, rolling around on the lawn. People have been locked up for less. I noticed that Dad was anxious. He didn't talk about how he felt or what he was thinking. Much was at stake, not only whether he would dare make the jump, but also his future at the University

---

1.   Today, Ram-air canopies are used right from the very first jump. The instructor on the ground stays in radio contact with the student and guides him to a soft landing.

of Lund. All his recent grant applications had been rejected and he had even heard rumors about "retirees" being "too old, not worth putting their money on." Dad was going to prove them wrong by becoming Scandinavia's oldest skydiver.

The day before the jump, Dad and his fellow students had the opportunity to show that they had truly mastered PLFs, emergency procedures, and exit technique. They were asked to do four perfect landings from the swing under the watchful eyes of two instructors. Dad passed the test with flying colors, which was a big relief as this had been the most difficult part of the training. He was then strapped in a harness with a reserve chute on the abdomen. The purpose was to simulate an emergency situation and ensure the students acted correctly. Skuris asked Dad to imagine a jump from the airplane when the canopy did not open at all.

"What's your solution?" he wanted to know.

Dad grabbed the reserve ripcord, closed his legs tightly, and resolutely pulled the ripcord. This was the correct action for a total malfunction, the terrifying situation when no part of the canopy deploys. After practicing a few more emergencies, it was time for the exit test. Dad climbed into the airplane mock-up and took his position. On Skuris' command he jumped forcefully and landed in the foam below. He was required to practice several times before his exits were approved. After passing all the practical tests, only the theoretical ones remained. The instructors wanted to make sure the students had not misunderstood anything which could have dangerous consequences in the air. Dad and his three fellow students passed the written test and Skuris and the chief instructor declared them ready for their first jump. The rest of the day was spent preparing the gear for the next day's jump.

When my mother and I arrived at Rinkaby field just south of Kristianstad, Dad was already set to go. An instructor had checked his gear and calibrated the AAD (Automatic Activation Device). This little box on the side of the reserve chute container has saved many lives. The AAD works with the help of a pressure gauge and is activated if the jumper descends past 1000 feet in freefall without a functioning canopy.

Dad waved to us as he stepped into the small Cessna-205 which would take the students to the jump altitude of 2000 feet. The pilot taxied to the runway and we watched the little plane take off with a buzzing sound. Dad would be the last to jump. An instructor standing next to me said the plan was to make two jump runs, with two students jumping each time. I followed the plane with my eyes as it ascended to 2000 feet. Suddenly I noticed a black spot falling from the plane and ten seconds later another spot. Two of the students had taken the leap into the skydivers' world. I was fascinated by the beautiful sight and thought to myself, "I'm gonna try that some day."

While I was daydreaming, Dad's turn had come. The airplane approached from the south. I lied down on the ground to see better. I barely had time to see him fall from the plane before the canopy bloomed open. Dad's canopy. He had done it: after a freefall of about 165 feet his canopy deployed according to plan. But the landing still remained. It looked as if he would land at the end of the field. At about 150 feet, I could see how Dad prepared for landing. The wind was calm and the canopy was coming practically straight down. Dad landed softly on the sun-dried field of grass.

He picked up the canopy and began walking toward the hangar where he was supposed to pack it up. We met him halfway. Mom and Dad hugged each other for a long time; Mom relieved that her husband was still alive, Dad excited over what he had accomplished at his age. I asked him how he felt about the jump and he answered with a huge smile. As it turned out, he had no recollection from the moment after he left the airplane until he was hanging safely beneath the deployed canopy.

Skuris had told us he had yet to meet someone who remembered details from their first freefall. The brain is too busy dealing with all the new impressions. It suddenly finds itself in unknown territory and needs some time to adjust. Reflexes have to take over in an emergency situation, drawing on the exhaustive training before the first jump. Dad told us the descent below the canopy was one of the highlights of the jump. He admired the beautiful view and enjoyed the quiet atmosphere, which he described as "strange." The canopy did not give the faintest sound as it slowly approached the ground. The difference between the jumps in Belgium in 1944 and his first jump in Rinkaby was that he didn't have to worry about being shot by German soldiers.

In the hangar, Skuris congratulated Dad on his first jump. Dad, in turn, thanked Skuris for all his help as well as moral support during the course. His three fellow students had also successfully completed their jumps and were packing their parachutes in the hangar. Dad felt satisfied with his day's work. He had proven to himself that he could still be counted on. He was still able to accomplish things that seemed impossible in other people's eyes. He had also shown the scientific community in Lund that a retiree can be active and productive.

A month after Dad's first jump, the magazine *Svensk Fallskärmssport* (Swedish Skydiving) published a four page article about his jump in Rinkaby. "This is the story of the Grand Old Man of Skåne," they wrote. One photo showed Dad as a young paratrooper in Europe, while another showed him as he climbed into the airplane in Rinkaby. The reporter wondered why a 69-year-old retiree would voluntarily jump from an airplane and Dad answered with conviction, "To show that life is not over at 69. To show that a lack of flexibility can be remedied with determination and training. To show that seemingly impossible feats can be overcome by positive thinking." The article concluded with a poem, "Night Jump in Georgia," which Dad wrote in 1944 while training as a paratrooper at Fort Benning, Georgia.

His colleagues at the Business Economics and Management Department in Lund congratulated him. Those who had doubted his abilities sat quietly by themselves. Dad sent copies of the *Svensk Fallskärmssport* article to the president of the University of Lund, as well as to institutions where he had applied for grants. It did not take long before he could move into his own office at the Business Management Department, compliments of the president, and the grant applications were suddenly approved.

Dad made a total of eight jumps with Skydive Skåne. Finally, during a downwind landing, he suffered a back injury. After wearing a back brace for two months, he was advised by his doctor to quit. Still, he visited his friends at Rinkaby every month. He often talked about the strong sense of camaraderie shared by the skydivers. Plumbers, welders, and electricians jumped alongside doctors, lawyers, and engineers. Everybody dressed the same in sweat suits and T-shirts. They got together for the sole purpose of skydiving and in the evenings they shared a sauna and cooked a meal together.

I accompanied Dad to the drop zone many times. I would sit by the hangar watching the parachutes floating down from all directions. Now and then I would enter the hangar and carefully study the jumpers when they packed their gear. When the airplane came in for fuel, I would climb inside. Sitting in the doorway, I would imagine getting ready to jump. The smell of aviation fuel evoked feelings of both excitement and fear.

Hooked

My first skydive was from a small sports plane, a Cessna-205, a few days before my eighteenth birthday. I was very nervous in the hours leading up to the jump, but strangely enough, I forgot all about it as soon as I got on the plane. The airplane was 25 years old and had previously been flown in Ethiopia for the Red Cross. To jump, you had to grasp the wing strut and pull yourself out onto a step facing the prop blast. This was already a difficult maneuver because of the wind, and the fear of the first jump only complicated things. I was lucky to be able to watch three of my classmates jump and survive before it was my turn.

I took a deep breath when the jumpmaster called me to the open door. "It's now or never," I thought. He helped me move to the gaping hole; the parachutes were very cumbersome, making it difficult to move without assistance. At the "Ready!" command I grabbed the strut with my left hand and followed quickly with my right hand. When I felt confident I wouldn't fall, I put my left foot on the step and let the right leg hang in the air. The roar of the engine and the prop blast made it difficult to hear, so I watched the jumpmaster's lips for the final command. The instant he yelled, "Go!" I let go of the strut, arched, and spread my arms and legs.

I fell at least 160 feet before the canopy opened; it felt like I was tumbling into a black hole, unable to control the fall in any way. The parachute took only a split second to open. I took a little time to congratulate myself on being brave enough to jump from 2000 feet, then concentrated on my next job: steering. I searched anxiously for the windsock on the ground, indicating the direction and speed of the wind. When I finally spotted it, I realized I was moving away from the drop zone and the landing area. I grabbed the steering toggles and turned the canopy around. Now I had a little time to enjoy the landscape below. Soon enough, however, the parachute and I closed in on the ground and I had to concentrate again. When I thought I was about 165 feet above ground, I prepared for landing. I reminded myself not to look down, keeping my eyes on the horizon to avoid pointing my toes on touchdown. My feet hit the ground a few seconds before I expected it. I rolled, then stood up as quickly as possible. That was when the adrenaline rush of excitement hit me for the first time.

My jumpmaster met me at the hangar and welcomed me into the skydivers' world. Only ten percent of the students in any particular class stay with it after one year. Most of them never get over the fear every beginner feels before a jump. I vowed to continue the sport, as I was excited by the thought of freefalling thousands of feet in the air.

Two weekends later I was ready for my first manual jump and I was terribly nervous. This time I had to decide for myself when to deploy the parachute. My first eight jumps had been "static line" jumps where my only preoccupation was maintaining correct body position during the short freefall. The parachute was deployed automatically with the help of the static line fastened inside the airplane. When the static line was pulled tight, the canopy was released from its container.

This time my life would be in my own hands. Instead of the static line, there was a metal ripcord on the right side of the harness. Pulling the ripcord released the three chute-retaining pins and deployed the canopy. Another difference was that the freefall would increase to five seconds. I had to freefall between two and five seconds in a stable, face-to-earth position in order to get the jump approved. The principle is simple: a good arch is necessary to remain in this basic freefall position. Arching makes a person automatically fall face-to-earth, the so-called box position. A good analogy is a shuttlecock, which always lands the same way. Maintaining this position is not as easy as it sounds. Practice is the key to achieving the correct body position instinctively. Forget the arch, and the result is immediate: you will spin through the air like a top.

I practiced locating the vital ripcord before entering the airplane. With my eyes closed, I imagined deploying the canopy, grabbing the ripcord with my right hand, and pulling it forcefully. An instructor counseled me before the jump and told me that few skydivers freefall more than two seconds during their first manual jump. Very few fall the maximum five seconds for reasons such as fear and poor body position. "When your life depends on pulling a metal handle, many people pull it the second after they jump." I decided to do my best to freefall for five seconds. To keep track of the time, you count out loud, "Arch thousand, look thousand, reach thousand, pull thousand." On "look thousand," locate the ripcord, on "reach thousand," grip it tightly, on "pull thousand," pull. The altimeter on my reserve chute was also new to me. It was separated into fields, showing zero to 12,500 feet. An easily visible red line at the 2000-foot mark reminds you it's time to wake up and deploy the main canopy. According to Swedish regulations, the canopy must be deployed at 2000 feet regardless of exit altitude. To achieve this, the ripcord should be pulled at 2,500 feet in order to take into account the time for the canopy to inflate fully.

Sitting comfortably in the Club's aircraft, which we named Ester, I tried to rid my brain of anything that did not relate to my jump. I visualized the jump several times with my eyes closed. The ascent to the jump altitude of 3000 feet gave me ample time to go through every detail of the jump, from exit to pull, several times. The ability to visualize the jump mentally is an important part of skydiving. Once we reached an altitude of 3000 feet, the jumpmaster directed the pilot to the exit point. My jumpmaster asked the pilot to reduce the engine power by yelling, "Cut," then looked at me and said, "Okay."

My turn was up. Concentrating on the jump, I climbed out and positioned myself on the step. I took a deep breath and let go. This was my freefall. "Arch thousand, look thousand, reach thousand," I counted out loud to myself. Looking toward the spot where the ripcord was supposed to be, I discovered it wasn't there. Unfortunately, there was no time to figure out what had happened to it. I had to do something, and quickly. My right hand touched something which felt like a wire. With the wire between my forefinger and thumb, I pulled hard. What a relief when the canopy deployed.

The jumpmaster did not approve my first manual jump. He told me I had fallen in a correct body position for three seconds, and then suddenly started tumbling around in the air. Besides, when the canopy deployed, I was falling in a back-to-earth position. All together, I had been in freefall for ten seconds, twice the maximum time. A jumpmaster who happened to be watching my freefall with binoculars knew what had happened and commended me for my actions. The ripcord had come loose from its pocket during the exit and positioned itself on my back. Thanks to my long arms I was able to reach the wire attached to the ripcord. I had been very close to using my reserve chute.

Later the same day, I made two more jumps from the same altitude, both of which were approved. In the evening, I followed the old jumping tradition of buying a case of beer for the rest of the gang. This rule is actually written into the unofficial international regulations, explaining the various occasions jumpers are to provide a case: the first manual jump, reserve pull, the one-hundredth jump, the first naked jump, and birthdays, just to mention a few. The jumper carries the case into the clubhouse, places it on a table and yells, "CASE!" for everybody to hear. The resulting mayhem looks like a stampede; everybody in the room comes running, eager to secure their can of beer. I have never seen a case last longer than ten seconds during my entire skydiving career.

The camaraderie among the members of the skydiving club was fantastic. We got to know each other very well, despite only meeting on weekends. The clubhouse became a home away from home, where we cooked meals, enjoyed the sauna, and tended to the parachutes and our aircraft, Ester. Of course, bailing out of airplanes was still the main activity. Appearance and where you came from were of less importance. "The Pink Panthers" was the club's most successful skydiving team and consisted of an anesthesiologist, a welder, a newspaper carrier, and a gardener. The club became my second home and it was sometimes hard to choose between my parents in Lund and the skydiving club in Rinkaby. I had gone jump crazy. My poor mother worried every time I left for Rinkaby. She read all the fatality reports and was concerned I would get hurt.

My mother often asked if I wasn't going to quit the sport now that I had proven that I had the guts. I explained that skydiving had become a lifestyle for me. I had found a sport which fulfilled all my dreams about adventure and excitement. The ironic thing was that it was my mother who made it possible for me to enter the world of adventures. I was only 17 when I made my first jump and needed parental permission for admission to the jump course. I charmed my mother for two months before she finally gave in and signed the permission slip. My father would have signed immediately had I asked him, but I wanted my mother on my side, too, even if reluctantly. The affirmation came on my eighteenth birthday, when my parents contributed 1,500 Swedish *kronor* toward the purchase of my first parachute. It was blue and yellow and I named it Åke.

I made 100 jumps during my first year as an active skydiver. When I had mastered freefalling in a stable face-to-earth position for more than 20 seconds, I began practicing turns. The idea was to learn to control my body during freefall. I would start each jump with a 12-second freefall to reach terminal velocity. The faster you fall, the easier it is to execute precise movements in freefall. Of course, there is a limit to how fast you can fall, set by the laws of physics. The fastest a person can freefall in a face-to-earth position is 120 mph, which is reached after 12 seconds. It is possible to fall faster, but in a different position: with the head down, arms alongside the body, and legs together, a speed of 250 mph can be reached.

To make sure I would return to my original position and not turn too much, I locked my eyes on an object on the ground. It could be a house, a corner of a grove of trees or something similar. I turned a quarter of a circle to the left by pressing down my left hand. To stop the turn, I compensated in the same manner with my right hand a little before the turn was complete. I returned to my starting point and then made the same turn but to the right. Having mastered quarter turns, I got the go-ahead to make 360-degree turns. The challenge of a 360 is stopping the turn at the right moment without continuing another 180 degrees. One turn to the left, stop! One turn to the right, stop! One turn to the left, stop! Later, I learned how to make forward and backward loops, freefall in a stable back-to-earth position, and make barrel rolls.

In preparation for Relative Work (RW) jumps, which are formation jumps with any number of participants from two to 250, I was taught the tracking position. This body position is comparable with the ski jumper's position after he leaves the ski jump: arms alongside the body, hands cupped, toes stretched, head and shoulders against the chest, and swish!! off you go, horizontally. The more participants in a jump, the earlier you have to start tracking. Four jumpers may start tracking at 3000 feet, eight jumpers at 3,600 feet, etc. When jumping in big formations with 50 to 60 skydivers, it is important to stay disciplined and within one's own jump area while tracking or there could be serious trouble. With both horizontal and vertical speed, crashing into another skydiver could be fatal.

My tracking jumps went well and I was ready for my first RW jump. For the first time, I would be able to see another skydiver next to me during freefall. My jump partner was the jumpmaster Stefan Olsson, a.k.a. Sol. Sol had made 700 jumps and was considered an experienced relative work jumper. We were to jump from 10,000 feet simultaneously and my job was to fly up to Stefan and carefully grab his arms. At 4000 feet, we were going to break the formation, track, and deploy our chutes. I wrote the following in my log book after the jump: "I docked with Sol and was rewarded with a big wet kiss, broke away at 4000 feet, tracked, my goggles slid down, didn't see anything, therefore bad tracking." I failed the jump because I did not track far enough. With my goggles on my chin and an air speed of 120 mph, I was practically blind. My eyes watered and I decided to deploy my canopy.

Now I could understand why experienced skydivers had told me that relative work was a fantastic experience. To freefall at a speed of 120mph for more than a minute together with good friends, is something I wish everybody could experience at least once in their lives. The sight of a friend's face distorted by the strong wind can make even the grumpiest person laugh until he cries. Those who jump with their mouths open look like blowfish when the wind fills the oral cavity. After seeing themselves in a photo taken during freefall, they usually keep their mouths shut. With the mouth shut, the wind presses the cheeks up toward the eyes, giving the jumper a square devil's face.

What intrigued me most about relative work was the possibility of controlling body movement during freefall. Stretch your legs and you move forward, stretch your arms and you back up. Even the falling speed can be controlled by arching. The more you arch, the faster you fall. This is especially important in formations with other skydivers where everybody needs to be on the same level. If one skydiver falls a foot and a half above the rest of the group, a little extra arch will bring him on level with the others before he docks. To further complicate relative work, nature makes sure people come in different sizes and shapes. Tall and slim, short and plump, everybody has a different rate of fall. Theoretically, a stone and a feather fall with the same speed—in a vacuum. In freefall, air resistance becomes a factor. It takes several practice jumps for four people with varying body shapes to fall at the same speed without having to think about it. I made three more RW jumps the same day with experienced jumpers. My technique improved each time and I couldn't help comparing myself to a baby bird learning to fly. In the beginning, I was hesitant and overly cautious in my movements. Skydiving had reached yet another dimension in my eyes with my introduction to RW jumping. I had a whole new world to explore, a world I had previously only glimpsed from inside passenger planes, but which I now was about to explore in freedom, falling at high speed.

After my 69th skydive, I took part in a boogie. This is not a dance, but a skydivers' carnival. My first boogie was the "Hercules Boogie '82." The organizers had managed to convince the Swedish Airforce to rent out one of its C-130 Hercules transports. A Hercules has the capacity to hold 20 tons of cars or light armored vehicles. Fill it with skydivers and there is room for 85. The airplane has a wide ramp that can be lowered, which means that 25 jumpers can leave the plane simultaneously. A Hercules ascends to 13,000 feet within only 10-12 minutes, something which is greatly appreciated by skydivers. Jumpers from 15 countries were registered for the boogie and a total of 600 skydivers were gathered at the same place for four days. We slept in tents or trailers set up in the drop zone. One corner housed the Dutch jumpers, another corner the British and another the French. The Hercules turbo engines roared from early morning till late at night. In the evenings, we entertained ourselves by drinking copious amounts of beer and with activities such as juggling, building human pyramids, playing Frisbee and kicking around Hackey sacks.

We had also rented an F-28 from the Swedish airline Linjeflyg. Linjeflyg was somewhat hesitant when the organizers insisted on removing all the seats, carpets, and the airplane door. Skydivers sit on the airplane floor to squeeze in as many as possible, and doors only get in the way and cause problems. I especially enjoyed adding new aircraft to my jumping repertoire. In Skåne, there was only Ester, a Cessna-205 with room for five skydivers. I had also jumped from a Cessna-206 a few times, and now I could add two more models to my list, the C-130 Hercules and the F-28 Fokker Fairchild.

More than 4000 jumps were made in four days and not a single serious accident was reported. My funniest memory from the boogie was when a group of girls suddenly began undressing inside the plane at an altitude of 12,000 feet. They removed every single piece of clothing until they stood there in their birthday suits, wearing only their parachutes. I think it goes without saying that we applauded their initiative wholeheartedly. The ramp was lowered at 13,000 feet and they all jumped out. The military jumpmaster, not used to seeing such scantily clad ladies in the aircraft, could not take his eyes off the show. Their reception upon landing was more than enthusiastic.

New Friends in High Places

Most of my friends were students at the University of Lund. I considered studying journalism, but didn't have the grades needed for admission. Nothing else in the course catalog interested me enough to sign up for three to four years of studies. After much consideration, I made the decision to move abroad.

Paris was the natural choice when I thought about the wonderful Christmas my family spent in the Loire Valley when I was 15. That was when, for the first time, I fell in love with a French specialty after visiting the beautiful châteaux of Chenonceau, Chambord, and Chaumont—oysters! In Sweden, I had heard terrible stories about how the French ate live oysters. I imagined the poor oysters crawling back and forth on the plate, crying for help. Now, with an oyster tray on the table in front of me, I realized that they were calmly lying there, waiting to be eaten. If they were alive, they didn't show it. I ate a dozen *fines de claire* No. 5, which is still my favorite type of oyster for both size and taste. Gulp! Mmmmmm. Gulp! Mmmmm.

I sent letters to 200 Swedish companies with branch offices in France in the hopes of landing a job. It didn't take long before I received answers to my letters; unfortunately all of them negative. The tone of the letters was courteous but firm. "Dear Mr. Dedijer, we thank you for your interest but are sorry to inform you that we do not have an appropriate position to offer. We wish you good luck in your continued search. Sincerely..." After more than 50 negative responses I received a positive reply from Gambro, a Swedish kidney dialysis equipment manufacturer. I had no idea what my position would be within the company, but suspected some type of office work. I was to work for Gambro for three months, filling in for a secretary on vacation. The housing problem was solved when the woman who had hired me wrote another letter in which she "was happy to inform" me that Gambro had arranged for a room near La Bastille. My wage had been set at the minimum wage in France, 5000 francs a month. To be on the safe side, I asked my mother to help me buy a nice dress shirt and matching tie. I might as well make a good first impression. As if one good piece of news was not enough, another positive answer arrived, this time from Facit, wondering if I would be able to begin as a trainee by the end of September. The reply from Facit was written on a small white card in almost illegible handwriting, and signed by Stellan Horwitz, the company CEO. Considering all the things I wanted to take with me, I decided to travel by train. I reserved a cot in a sleeping car so I could sleep away the train ride. My mother came with me to the station to wave good-bye. It was a sad goodbye because I had no idea when I would see her again.

The train ride was fast and painless. When I arrived at Gare du Nord, one of the six railroad stations in Paris, I took a taxi to my new address on Rue Sedaine. The summer of '83 was very hot in Europe; pearls of sweat trailed down my back as I sat on the vinyl seat of the taxi. The taxi pulled up in front of an old run-down building. I got out and stared at my new home. I rang the landlord's door-bell and introduced myself. A grumpy woman in hair curlers glared at me and handed me some keys. "Top floor, down the hall, under the roof!" she yelled before slamming the door shut.

"Oh well," I thought. "Now I know which doorbell not to ring again." The hallway light on the top floor was burnt out and I got the impression I was moving into a house ready for demolition. I knocked on one door at the end of the hall. No answer. Carefully, I inserted one of the keys in the lock. The key turned easily, but the door seemed to be stuck. I gave it a hard shove and fell headfirst into my rented room.

The heat was unbearable, a real sauna. I put my bags in a corner and began inspecting my new home. It didn't take long. I estimated the room to be nine foot square. An old, well used armoire, missing both shelves and hangers, was in a corner. The rest of the furniture consisted of a wooden chair and a bed which would not even have been big enough for Napoleon Bonaparte. I made the strangest discovery last: the kitchen, toilet and sink were all squeezed into a space of less than ten square feet. Sitting on the toilet, I had the cooking burner 12 inches in front of me. Not very appetizing. The sink was so small only one hand could be washed at a time. There was no shower, but I was hoping to find a swimming pool in the neighborhood where I could wash up. I was very disap-pointed with the standards of Instrumenta Gambro's worker housing. How would I keep my food cold without a refrigerator? I certainly couldn't eat in res-taurants every night. I had many questions and few answers on my first evening in Paris.

The following day I went to Gambro's headquarters, located in the Ninth Arrondissement. I was surprised to see several scantily dressed women lined up like dolls on the street. It was not difficult to imagine what they were waiting for. I was also surprised to find that Gambro had chosen an area like this for their headquarters. A receptionist greeted me professionally and offered me coffee while I waited for my contact person. The reception area was nicely furnished and gave the impression of a successful company. A blond woman in high heels suddenly appeared and introduced herself so quickly I didn't catch her name. We walked through long hallways with nice, framed prints on the walls and stopped by a door marked with a brass sign. Before entering the room I tried to read the sign, but she was too fast. All I could see was the word *Directrice*. I sat down in the visitor's chair facing the desk. She welcomed me to Instrumenta Gambro and expressed her hope that I would enjoy my three months with the company. Then she delivered the sentence. With the precision of a machine, she gave the orders: "You begin work tomorrow. Show up at our warehouse 19 miles outside of Paris tomorrow morning at eight. You will work in the warehouse and load trucks. Your work hours are…"

I wasn't listening. I felt like the world had come to an end. A warehouse worker. I might as well throw away the shirt and tie I got from mom, unless, of course, I wanted to impress the truck drivers. The blond woman in front of me continued to talk, but she hàd lost me. She gave me a pile of forms which I filled out dutifully. Then I stood up and thanked her for…I didn't know what. I left the Gambro headquarters with the warehouse address in my hand. My mood was at rock-bottom.

I had set my alarm for six for my first day of work. I didn't want to be late. The subway brought me to Gare de l'Est, from where I took a bus, arriving in the suburb of Aulnay-sous-Bois forty minutes later. The warehouse was another 20 minutes walk from the bus stop. I had spent a total of an hour and a half getting to work. Gambro's warehouse was in an industrial area and my boss was Monsieur Salés. He offered me a beer and as we drank, he explained my duties. An 80-foot-long truck would arrive twice daily from Sweden or Germany. My job was to empty the truck with the help of an electric pallet jack and place the pallets in their appropriate slots in the warehouse. Once a day, another truck would come to pick up orders. I was to load the truck. The only variation in my duties would be the direction I moved the pallets, either in or out of a truck. Not used to hard physical labor, I felt exhausted after eight hours. I showered four times a week at the train station on my way home from work. After two months I had not been out a single night and had not made the acquaintance of a single interesting person.

When I entered the Irish pub The Silver Goblet one warm September evening in 1983, little did I suspect it would be the beginning of the adventure of my life; an adventure I had never dared to imagine. I chose a table in front of a big poster with the message "Guinness is good for your health," and ordered a pint. A small group of Frenchmen sitting at a table next to mine was deeply engaged in a political discussion. I did not pay any attention to them until I heard an American voice say, "You're nuts!" The American turned to the bar to order a drink and I decided to take the opportunity to initiate a conversation. I asked if I could buy him a beer and he accepted with a smile on his face. He sat down at my table and introduced himself as Scott Elder from Connecticut, USA, and seemed happy to meet someone who wanted to discuss beer instead of politics. Scott was handsome, above average height, muscular, and had dark brown hair, green eyes, and a long, straight nose.

Scott told me he had been working for Yves Saint-Laurent for almost two years, but I never did find out his exact position with the company. I got the impression that he had not talked to a foreigner for a long time and wanted to make up for it. Scott Elder's mother worked as a secretary and his father was a pilot for the American airline TWA. His face beamed when I told him I was from Sweden, and he suddenly started speaking Swedish with an American accent. *"Tycka du om vackra svensk flicka? Jag har bott i Lund i Skåne i ett år för att lära svenska!"* At first, since I was so used to hearing French all the time, I didn't realize he had spoken to me in my native tongue. Scott repeated the sentence in unbelievably correct Swedish, surprised that I hadn't understood him right off the bat. I couldn't believe my good luck: I walk into an Irish pub in Paris and run into an American who speaks Swedish, learned in my hometown of Lund. Scott explained he had spent a year in Sweden as an exchange student. The University of Lund's many connections with Scott's university in the United States made it the natural choice for him. We each ordered another beer and continued our discussion. Not only did Scott speak Swedish, he also told me that he practiced skydiving, but had not jumped for three months. Scott probably expected me to react like a "whuffo"[1] and ask the classic question, "What happens if the chute doesn't open when you pull the handle?" Instead, I asked him how many jumps he had made and he looked at me curiously. I broke the silence by telling him I had made 180 jumps. Scott laughed out loud at this news and patted me on my shoulder in a friendly gesture. We both felt like we had known each other for years even though we had met only an hour before. Scott had made 250 skydives, counting about 100 in France. The bar was about to close for the night and the strong beer had made my brain a little fuzzy. Before we left, I asked Scott to write

---

1. A person who doesn't know anything about skydiving. Originated the day a farmer asked, "Wha' fo' you jump outta them airplanes fo'?"

down his address on a beer coaster. We decided to skydive together the following weekend at a drop zone just outside Paris.

My stomach harbored a few butterflies when I got out of bed the following Saturday, one week after my first meeting with Scott. I was nervous. I figured it was the knowledge that I was about to jump out of a plane again for the first time in quite a while that made my stomach protest. The pattern was that if I hadn't jumped for a few weeks, I would feel uneasy, a feeling which would usually disappear the moment I jumped from the plane. My previous jump had been in Rinkaby three months earlier. We had jumped from 10,000 feet and managed six formations in freefall before tracking off and deploying our chutes. One dose of freefall a month was an absolute minimum in order for me to maintain a calm and harmonious approach to life.

I was to meet Scott in his apartment at 42 Avenue de Saxe in the Seventh Arrondissement. I took the subway to the Ségur station and then walked the short distance to Avenue de Saxe. The door code was written on a small piece of paper which I carefully unfolded. As I entered the last digit of the code, the door clicked open and I stepped in. I quickly found Scott's apartment on the fourth floor as he, contrary to the custom in France, had a sign with his name on the door. It is a strange habit of the French not to post names on apartment doors, which often causes visitors to try two or three doors before they hit the right one.

I rang the doorbell and waited for Scott to open up. Half a minute later I rang the bell again. No answer. I banged on the thick wooden door with the palm of my hand until I was sure the entire building was awake. All in vain. I tried the door handle and to my surprise the door slowly opened. What was he doing? Did he have a woman in his bed or had he gone out for breakfast? I made my way through a dark hallway and entered a big room. A strange smell enveloped me, a mixture of sweat and booze. As my eyes adjusted to the darkness, I could see something moving under the covers; Scott was lost in a deep sleep. When I called his name, he poked his head out and asked, "Why did you get here so early?" He dragged himself out of bed and headed for the bathroom, offering me something to drink from the refrigerator. He must have had a real wild night to look like that, I thought.

As Scott washed away the signs of a sleepless night, I looked around his apartment. It was a paradise compared to my own. The apartment consisted of a bedroom of about 200 square feet, with a grand foyer, bathroom, small kitchen, and an enormous closet, one of the biggest closets I had ever seen. About twenty perfectly pressed suits hung in neat rows along both walls. It was obvious these were suits of the highest quality. Ties in every imaginable color and pattern were neatly organized on a shelf. I noticed several colorful collages on the walls, all signed YSL.

Scott reappeared after his shower totally naked with a towel draped around his neck. He now looked like an actual human being. When he was dressed, he collected his skydiving gear in a big sports bag: parachute, jumpsuit, helmet, altimeter, and goggles. Scott's friend Jean was already waiting in his car with the engine running when we came outside. I got comfortable in the backseat and closed my eyes to try to sleep, since I had not hit the sack until four in the morning after a hectic barhopping adventure. The drop zone was located about 60 miles east of Paris in the small village of La Ferté Gaucher. Fifty-five thousand jumps were made there during the 1983 season, compared to 30,000 jumps in Sweden during the same period.

It was with mixed emotions of enthusiasm and anxiety that I realized we were getting closer to the airfield. This time I was about to "skydive in French." It had taken me more than a year to learn all the special terminology in English; now I had to learn it in French. And it is common knowledge that the French are not very eager to speak English.

One drawback with big drop zones is that the wait between jumps can be long. Scott had jumped at La Ferté for more than a year and knew everybody worth knowing. Those who knew him well called him "*l'américain.*" The skydiving club owned three aircraft: two Pilatus Porters and one Twin Otter. The first type is manufactured in Switzerland, made to fly in the Swiss Alps. The plane ascends and descends quickly, which makes it one of the favorite planes for skydiving. If there is anything skydivers do not like, it is flying in slow planes which take forever to reach jump altitude. The Twin Otter is a twin engine turboprop with a capacity of 20 skydivers. It's made in Canada by De Havilland. It is also one of the more popular planes.

I made a few jumps with Scott and his French friends and felt almost immediately accepted by the other skydivers. For the first time I took part in a big formation of 20 skydivers, Scott and I and 18 Frenchmen. We jumped from the Twin Otter and built a beautiful formation. I knew everybody would watch the newcomer during freefall to see what he was capable of. Luckily, I did well in freefall and didn't bounce around or come down on top of one of the other skydivers. The formation was photographed by a freefalling photographer with a camera mounted on his helmet.

BASE

After two weekends jumping at La Ferté I was introduced to the cryptic abbreviation BASE. I was talking to a member of the British National RW team, Symbiosis, when he told me he had recently jumped from a 825-foot-high bridge. Immediately interested, I listened in amazement. After hearing his story I concluded he must have been crazy.

Let me explain. A skydiver always wears two parachutes, a main and a reserve. In the event of a major malfunction of the main canopy the skydiver jettisons it, preferably above 1000 feet, and deploys the reserve canopy. Below 1000 feet, you should avoid deploying the reserve canopy for the simple reason that there may not be enough time for it to deploy fully. Instead, you should try to land with the defective main canopy, if possible. The Englishman had jumped from a bridge so low that the reserve canopy could not have been used in an emergency situation. If a problem had developed with the main canopy, he would be headed for certain death. He called this BASE jumping, explaining that the sport originated with a BASE club founded in the United States. Entry to the club required jumps from a building, an antenna, a bridge, and a cliff. The English acronym for the four objects is BASE (Building, Antenna, Span, Earth).

Scott also must have been thinking about BASE jumping, because toward the end of September 1983, he asked if I would like to join him on a trip to Norway to jump from a cliff called Trollveggen. Was he kidding? I had already heard about a few people jumping from this 2000-foot cliff, but I didn't feel like risking my life on a crazy jump from an isolated cliff, so I declined Scott's offer. Scott was going to the small village of Åndalsnes, near Trollveggen, along with Christophe, a Frenchman of Polish heritage. Christophe had made the long trip once before by himself. He had set up his tent on the campground. His brought his parachute, so the purpose of his trip was undoubtedly to make a jump from Bruraskaret. The climb from Trollstigen, the starting point for the mountain paths leading to Brurarskaret, takes two to three hours for an untrained city-dweller. The terrain varies between gravel paths and slippery snow depending on the season. The jump site is difficult to find with only a map, but Åndalsnes is full of young men hoping for the chance to watch someone jump from the 2000-foot cliff and therefore happy to show the way.

But Christophe was determined to find the jump site by himself. He spent more than a week searching for Bruraskaret and then a day and a night in his sleeping bag dangerously close to the ledge. The next day he returned down the same way he came and took the train back to Paris. His decision not to jump may seem like natural behavior, but Christophe was a strange man. He was afraid to talk on the telephone as he believed some obscure cult was after him and he was certain his apartment was bugged. His drapes were always drawn so the supposed pursuers wouldn't be able to tell if he was home or not. Scott and Christophe left at the end of September, when the weather can be bad in the Norwegian mountains. Several people had advised Scott not to jump from Trollveggen. A Frenchman by the name of Philippe had almost convinced him to cancel the trip by telling him about how he spent 16 hours on a ledge 1,300 feet above ground after leaping from Trollveggen. He had crashed straight into the mountain wall and amazingly managed to land on a ledge measuring only 20 square feet. The unsuccessful jump almost cost him his life. It did cost him 100,000 Norwegian *kroner* in fees required by the Norwegian government to pay for the rescue effort. The Norwegian Air Force sent a helicopter which managed to pull him to safety after some dramatic maneuvering.

I thought about Scott every day after he left. Although I didn't know him very well yet, I was very concerned about him. I really admired his courage. This would be his first BASE jump and he didn't have much more than his intense enthusiasm going for him. Ten days after his departure I received a postcard. "Hello Jevto. I have made three jumps and plan to spend the rest of the time drinking Norwegian beer. Scott." I was enormously relieved. Scott had accomplished the letter E in the acronym BASE.

When we met again in Scott's apartment on Avenue de Saxe he described his jumps in detail. He had ended up headfirst in the first two jumps, unintentionally falling back-to-earth and facing the cliff. Scott told me he had never before been so scared as when he realized he was falling on his back, 1,300 feet above ground, surrounded by unforgiving cliff walls. Somehow he escaped the frightening situation unharmed. The third jump went well.

Slowly but surely, my feelings about BASE jumping were beginning to change. It still seemed highly dangerous and totally crazy, but at the same time, something about it attracted me. Scott talked enthusiastically about the quiet, the fear, the acceleration, and the adrenaline rush. He began corresponding with a man by the name of Carl Boenish in California. Carl Boenish was known as an excellent freefall photographer. He had produced several funny and entertaining films about skydiving, including the well known "Sky Dive!" He was without doubt the world's leading freefall photographer during the 70s and early 80s. He always found new ways of shooting photographs and films, attaching his cameras on airplanes, on his chest or his head, and even inside canopies.

Carl had a few good friends who, like Carl, had tired of skydiving from airplanes and wanted to try something new. In 1978, inspired after hearing of previous jumps from El Capitan in Yosemite National Park, they made several successful jumps from the well known 3000-foot cliff. Climbers scale the steep and physically tiring rock wall often, but Carl and his friends made it the birthplace of an entire new sport. Eventually, they returned to Yosemite for more. Soon they discovered they were surrounded by enticing jump sites. TV towers, bridges, buildings...

This newfound wealth of jump sites inspired Carl to come up with the guidelines for a new sport, BASE jumping. Carl and his wife Jean teamed up with two friends, Phil Smith and Phil Mayfield, to found the BASE club. Jumping from each of the four types of fixed objects would earn the jumper membership and the right to wear the BASE jumper insignia on the sleeve. The four friends jumped from all the bridges, buildings, antennas, and cliffs they could find. Carl filmed as Jean jumped and vice-versa. They jumped from an office building in downtown Houston at daybreak, went to work in the morning, and made yet another jump after work. Realizing the need for a somewhat different technique than in classical skydiving from aircraft, they met in the evenings and discussed new ways to pack the parachute, exit techniques, and lowest possible "safe" exit altitude. Phil Smith, Phil Mayfield, Carl Boenish and Jean Boenish thus became the first four members in the BASE club. These four people were the pioneers of a very dangerous sport, a sport which ordinary, honest citizens watch with both admiration and utter disbelief.

Carl provided Scott with advice via mail on how to make his BASE jumping as safe as possible. The problem was that there were only ten BASE jumpers in all of Europe, making it difficult to reach someone who could suggest suitable objects for jumping. No member directory was available at the time and the Web had not yet been invented. One evening after reading one of Carl's letters, Scott told me the reason he ended up on his back during his first two jumps from Trollveggen. He had jumped off the cliff using the same technique as in skydiving from an airplane: headfirst. Carl wrote that in BASE jumps, the best technique is to carry the head high with the chest toward the horizon. "Otherwise you risk flipping over, ending up in a back-to-earth position," the letter ended. I pointed out to Scott that he had been very lucky to avoid injury. He laughed heartily and told me he was used to learning things the hard way, but promised to be more careful in the future.

Scott had been working for Yves Saint-Laurent for more than a year, but he had still not found his place within the company. He had tried to find an interesting position, but instead he had been sent from one department to another. He started out as an assistant to the assistant director of marketing, and then was sent to the perfume department for a short time. He finally realized he did not have a real future with the company. It did not help that he was a personal friend of Yves himself. He just did not fit into the wealthy, hysterical, schizophrenic world of fashion. Despite this, Yves often invited him to dinner at his apartment on Rue Babylone in the Seventh Arrondissement. A rumor that Scott was Yves' new lover circulated viciously in the hallways of the fashion world. Tabloids are often criticized for spreading false rumors, but the fashion world's own blabbermouths are just as fond of gossip. Had I not personally known Scott, I might have believed them. He lived in an apartment owned by Yves Saint-Laurent and rent, electricity, and telephone were paid for by the company. One Christmas, he was invited to Yves' Summer Palace in Marrakech, and he spent several weekends at Yves' weekend home in Deauville on the coast of Normandy. He received many beautiful collages made by Yves himself from colorful cardboard. I think Scott was one of the few people who appealed to Yves as an ordinary person, and he appreciated him for that. Yves was constantly surrounded by people who did everything in their power just to be noticed. According to Scott, he never knew who was honest and straightforward or who was faking it. People were even beginning to show jealousy toward Scott because Yves spent so much time in his company.

The situation was intolerable. Most of all, Scott wanted to live a normal life. He was tired of the constant parties which did not contribute to his personal well-being, but only gave him headaches and stomach pains. Scott left the hectic fashion scene in October 1983. He decided to take a month off and devote his time to painting and studying Italian. As an artist, his main interest was paper collages, but he also produced beautiful watercolors of various sights in Paris. His bedroom floor served as a studio. Scott had purchased a beginner's course in Italian which included a study book and three cassette tapes. The study book did not get used very much, but with the help of the tapes, Scott soon spoke decent Italian with an admittedly heavy American accent.

Scott and I were becoming close friends. We were alike in many ways, sharing the same habits, both good and bad. I slowly but surely got to know the real

Scott: a guy in badly worn jeans, a cold beer in his hand, preferably the Chinese beer Tsingtao, and his banjo. Without the banjo, Scott was lost. He had been playing since he was fifteen and was quite accomplished. I tried many times to follow his fingers as they quickly moved across the thin strings, but always had to give up when my head started spinning. Playing the banjo was Scott's way to relax. He would sit down in his favorite spot on the big bed and play for hours. He often played for me and then asked my opinion. Through Scott, I got acquainted with bluegrass music, which sounded to me like a mix between country and rock. (Please forgive me if I just said something stupid. I didn't do well in music at school.)

One evening, after a long day in the warehouse, I visited Scott in his apartment. He welcomed me with a cold bottle of Tsingtao and the words, "Come in, I have something to show you." One wall in his apartment was covered with postcards, photos, small souvenirs, and posters. He pointed to a postcard showing a skyscraper I thought looked familiar, and asked, "Well, what do you think?" I answered the building was impressive and almost beautiful, but to me, a skyscraper was just a skyscraper. He turned the postcard over and showed me the text, *"Hauteur, 210 m"* (Height 210 m). It suddenly dawned on me: he was suggesting we jump from the building!

The Montparnasse Tower was a 15 minute walk from Scott's apartment. Anyone who has visited Paris has seen the Montparnasse Tower, which along with the Eiffel Tower dominates the Paris skyline. And Scott was considering jumping from this office building! I had no problem declining his offer again, just as I had done with Trollveggen. I simply did not feel mentally ready for such a risky jump, a jump which could be my last. It seemed a bit too crazy to me, but Scott needed help organizing and planning his jump, so I offered to help in any way I could.

About the time that Scott began preparing for his adventure, I finally changed jobs. My stint as a trainee at Instrumenta Gambro was over. It was a tremendous relief. The job had been physically exhausting and mind-numbingly boring, and the commute to and from the warehouse long. The best thing about my three months at Gambro was that I had come to realize how hard life as a warehouse worker is. My coworkers threw me a small farewell party on my last day. We had become good friends and they wanted to say goodbye in their own way. They provided beer and gave me a parting gift. When I opened the package on the bus to Paris I was a little surprised; properly wrapped in brown paper was a men's magazine with what I considered a very vulgar cover. A white card included with the gift read, "Just so you won't forget the French culture." The card was signed by all the warehouse workers.

My first day at Facit was promising. I was hired as an assistant to a pretty, young, dynamic woman by the name of Ylva Berthelson who was in charge of Facit's finances. Ylva was from Sweden and had lived in France for ten years. Her style was more French than Swedish: she used her hands and arms when she talked, was very straightforward, arrived late for work, and raised her voice a lot. My job was to make sure she had all the sales statistics, diagrams, and various other papers containing numbers at her fingertips. I was well received by the staff from the beginning which made me feel very comfortable. Facit's headquarters were located in Colombes, a suburb northwest of Paris. It took me just over an hour to get to work. But now I had a housing problem. I had to vacate my room since I no longer worked for Gambro.

Early one morning, it seemed as if the room had decided to take revenge on me for leaving. I heard a muffled bang followed by the sound of rushing water. I jumped out of bed and checked the "bathroom." The water pipe leading to the wash basin had broken in two and the water rushed out on the floor with unbelievable force. I tried in vain to plug the pipe with towels and rags. After a couple of minutes of this, there was a knock on the door: the neighbors. Water was coming through their bedroom ceiling and what was going on here? I ran downstairs to the landlady, to whom I had not spoken since my arrival, to ask for help. She looked at me with the same disdain as the first time we met and questioned my sanity as I had awoken her at six o'clock on a Sunday morning. A muscular man suddenly appeared from behind the door and introduced himself as the landlady's husband. After much convincing he agreed to take a look at the leak. Needless to say both the bed and armoire were floating in water by this time. He stopped the leak and returned to bed.

I felt no remorse as I packed my bags, but was concerned about finding a new place to live. Scott wouldn't mind taking me in for a while, but sooner or later I would have to find my own place. A friend of Scott's who had a room for rent heard I was looking for a place to live. The address was 15 Rue Pérignon in the Fifteenth Arrondissement. I asked her to wait while I checked a map of Paris and to my surprise discovered the street was only a few blocks from Scott's apartment. I hopped in a cab, met with the owner, and after a verbal agreement about the rent, got the keys to the apartment that very night.

The first night in my new home was like a night in a luxury hotel. The room was not much bigger than my previous apartment, but it was infinitely nicer. The furniture was intact and clean and there was even a bathtub. I had never seen anything like it: the bathtub was located in the middle of the room. You would think the plumber had consumed a bottle of whisky before installing it. Now I could shower when I wanted to and didn't have to visit the train station four times a week. My room was on the second story with a view of a dry cleaning business. A drain pipe stretched along the outside wall just by my window. This could come in handy if I happened to forget my keys, and I decided to always keep the window ajar. I had previous experience in climbing drain pipes and was good at it. The rent of 700 francs per month was low compared to the average rent in Paris, which was about 1100 francs for a room without a shower.

Scott and I started cooking together since we lived so close. I soon discovered that Scott cooked with the same vivid imagination as he created collages. We ate cod with grapes and beer sauce, beef with pears and ketchup, or simple dishes like spaghetti with Camembert. I tried to put a damper on his exuberant creativity when guests were invited. When I left for work in the mornings, Scott walked to the Montparnasse Tower. He had noticed a small number of guards patrolling the building and wanted to find out their habits and schedule before he dared a parachute jump from the roof. After a week of reconnaissance, he had gathered the intelligence he needed. He knew the number of guards and when and where they patrolled the building. After some consideration, he decided to jump from the east side of the deck on the 56th floor, right in front of the numerous tourists who took the elevator to the deck to admire the view.

I was sitting at my desk pondering the statistics of the month's sales of typewriters when the phone rang. It sounded like an internal call. I lifted the receiver and said, "Yes, hello." I had barely finished my "hello" when I was interrupted

"I did it. I jumped the son-of-a-bitch!"

"Huh?"

"Jevto, is that you? Don't you understand? I did it an hour ago! I got my B!"

Scott had done it. He had jumped from a 700-foot-high office building. I hung up, put my statistics aside and went to the coffee machine on the second floor. I wanted to be alone to celebrate Scott's victory. I sat down on a typical French café stool in orange plastic with a cup of coffee and thought about Scott's accomplishment. By his own free will he had jumped from a building in downtown Paris. He had not been threatened, lost a bet, or been pushed from the deck. No, he jumped for the fun of it. And it sounded like it was the most fun he had ever had. Naturally, I felt happy for him, happy that he survived, but also a bit disappointed that I hadn't been able to watch him tumble down.

After work, I went straight to Scott's apartment and found him sitting on the bed with his banjo. On a table by the bed was a big glass half full of whisky. We hugged and I congratulated him. I made myself comfortable on the bed with a glass of whisky and listened to Scott tell me about the jump. The guards had not posed a problem. They stuck to their well-established routine which Scott had studied carefully. The jump itself, however, almost ended in a catastrophe. Scott told me the parachute had not opened until 265 feet above ground and he landed only 15 seconds later. Immediately after leaping from the deck, he knew he had made a poor exit. He knew he was close to ending up on his back again, just as in his first two jumps from Trollveggen. He fell headfirst and seconds went by. The canopy did not want to open and Scott helped it along by shaking his body. With only three seconds left to the ground, it finally opened with a bang. Finding yourself alive when you think you're about to die is an exhilarating experience.

Scott had not followed Carl Boenish's advice regarding the exit. Instead of jumping with his head high and chest toward the horizon, he jumped headfirst, causing him to almost end up on his back. Knowing he was in deep trouble, Scott reacted by immediately throwing his pilot chute. A pilot chute is a small round canopy, 12 inches in diameter, which extracts the main canopy from its container. Located in a small pocket on the leg strap, it is deployed by grabbing it and releasing it in the air stream. When skydiving from an aircraft, the jumper deploys the pilot chute while falling at speeds of 120 mph. At such a high speed, the canopy opens very quickly. Scott had just begun accelerating when he threw the pilot chute, so it ended up stuck to his back like a useless rag. After four seconds of freefall, the wind finally grabbed hold of it and the canopy deployed. Carl had recommended that Scott freefall for at least three seconds before throwing the pilot chute, otherwise the pilot chute would risk getting caught in the turbulence behind him. Despite the mishap, Scott was now sitting safely on his bed, incredibly happy. When I asked him how it felt to jump from a building, he answered, "Jevto, if you want to know how it feels, jump yourself."

Scott's neighbor was an American woman who studied history at the Sorbonne. When she heard about the jump, she shook her head and commented, "Scott, you are a bored young man." She was absolutely right. He no longer had a job, spent all day in his apartment, and was separated by an entire ocean from his pretty girlfriend Maria. Originally from Thailand, Maria was studying in the United States and visited Europe only a couple of times a year. Scott missed her terribly. They spoke on the phone several times a week, usually resulting in Maria starting to cry, longing for Scott. He told her about his jump from the Montparnasse Tower which did not exactly calm her nerves. Scott's parents and family were very impressed when they heard about his adventure, but I don't believe they totally understood the difference between a BASE jump and a skydive. In any case, they were used to Scott's escapades and were not too worried. A friend of Scott's had photographed him hanging below his canopy with the Montparnasse Tower in the background. He sold the photo to a couple of newspapers and an article appeared the next day, titled, "American jumps from the pride of Paris!" What bothered the French the most was not that someone had actually jumped from the Montparnasse Tower, but that an American was the first to do it. He was even criticized by the skydivers at La Ferté, who obviously were jealous of his accomplishment. The French Skydivers' Association considered expelling him, thereby also preventing him from any further skydives in France. Luckily, the threat was not carried out.

Warning! Low Bridge

A thick envelope arrived in Scott's mailbox from Germany at the end of December 1983. It contained photos and tales of several jumps made by some of Scott's friends in Germany from a 610-foot-high bridge near Heidelberg. Scott had come to know the three Germans in a bar in Frankfurt and had written to them about his jump from the Montparnasse Tower. All three were skydivers and became very interested in Scott's BASE jump. He shared all available information regarding BASE jumping, which at that time was very little. They gleaned the most important information and had now each made a jump from a bridge.

Looking at their photos, I took a personal interest in BASE jumping for the very first time. It looked very simple. The bridge was located in a beautiful valley and surrounded by greenery. The Germans described how they had made a test jump with a 90-pound doll equipped with a parachute. The doll had been thrown from a 165-foot bridge. Before it reached the ground, the parachute had fully deployed. Therefore, they figured, just a little less than 165 feet was needed for the canopy to open. They made static line jumps, using the same technique beginners use during their very first jumps from airplanes. This is a relatively safe way to accomplish BASE jumps, even if it does not compare to the feeling of free-falling the way Scott had from the Montparnasse Tower.

Inside my head, a battle was raging between sound common sense and my desire for adventure. A little voice told me, "Jevto, think about your life and your family. Don't do anything so dangerous it could cost you your life."

Then I heard another voice, "Come on, a little adventure can't hurt you. It's been a long time since you did something exciting. It's time."

When I sat down and relaxed it didn't take long until everything seemed crystal clear. The adventurous side had won. Scott sat quietly on his bed, waiting for my answer. I looked him in the eye and said with conviction, "Scott, I want to BASE jump." He brightened like the sun and sat down beside me. We looked at the photos together and discussed how and when we would jump. To me, jumping from the bridge in Germany was the most attractive. I was not interested in jumping from the Montparnasse Tower, which I considered too dangerous at the time.

In my bed that night, I considered the implications of what I had gotten in to. "Jump from a bridge? I must be crazy," I thought. One Friday evening while sharing a few beers in a local bar with Scott, he told me he had met a guy by the name of Bernard at a drop zone near the Belgian border. Bernard and Scott immediately hit it off. According to Scott, Bernard was a whiz at telling jokes and they had challenged each other one night, surrounded by a jury of ten skydivers. Bernard told a story so hilarious that both Scott and the jury laughed till their bellies ached.

I suggested inviting Bernard to the apartment to find out if he truly was as funny as the rumors had it. I met Bernard a week later for the first time. He barged into Scott's apartment carrying a six-pack and greeting us with, *"Salut, ça va?"*

Bernard was of average height with an athletic build and had dark, curly hair and brown eyes. He was casually dressed in jeans, an oversized sweater and sneakers. All three of us sat down on Scott's bed and began to talk. Bernard told us he was 23 years old and lived with his parents in Bailly, not far from Versailles. He was a second-year archeology student, specializing in ancient South American Indian cultures. Our beer supply was depleted in 30 minutes and I rushed down to the corner store to replenish it. When I was once more ensconced in my spot on the bed, Bernard told us he had made 70 skydives, 30 of them during his military service with the French paratroopers. He had never made an RW jump and did not claim to be a truly experienced skydiver.

Scott and I showed him the photos from the German bridge and told him about our plans. We asked Bernard if he would consider driving our car to Germany if we paid his room and board. We were in need of a chauffeur who could take us to the bridge and then take care of the car after the jump. Bernard looked at us with surprise and said, "If I go, I jump. Otherwise, you'll have to find another driver." I could barely contain my excitement and surprise over Bernard's decision to do a BASE jump. He didn't have many jumps under his belt and had made his decision in less than a minute. He hadn't even asked how high the bridge was, and he was already determined to jump.

Shortly thereafter, we began planning our trip to Kochertalbrücke. Many things had to fall in place, the technical part not the least. We all had our own parachutes which was helpful. We considered what we had learned from Scott's mistakes at Trollveggen and the Montparnasse Tower. He had read an article in an American skydiving magazine, written by Carl Boenish, describing how bigger pilot chutes decrease the time it takes for the chute to deploy during BASE jumps. Scott brought the article to the French parachute manufacturer, Parachutes de France, to ask if they would sew three pilot chutes. They figured out what we planned to use the pilot chutes for and declined our request. Scott asked around until he found a small company willing to help us. We ordered three big pilot chutes in black nylon, twice the size of those used for normal jumps; we gave them the collective nickname "Mr. Black." We practiced exits in Scott's apartment by jumping from a low table onto his big bed. I must have made at least 200 practice jumps.

Not a day, not even an hour, went by when I didn't think about our trip. I wondered how Mom and Dad would react if they received a message that their son had died during a jump from a bridge. We spoke once or twice a week, but I never mentioned our plans, not wanting to worry them. I slept poorly. It took a long time to fall asleep, and I woke up several times a night. My dreams were always the same: I was plunging toward the ground at high speed without a parachute. I questioned my decision regarding the BASE jump. Did I really want to do this? What if I was injured and had to spend the rest of my life in a wheelchair? The week before our trip, I spoke to my boss at Facit, Ylva Berthelson, and requested the following Friday off. She asked me why, and I told her the truth: I was going to Germany to jump from a bridge. Ylva approved my request; I had a reputation as a joker at Facit, so I think Ylva considered the whole thing a prank.

On February 10, 1984, all three of us could be seen kneeling in the empty market square on Avenue de Saxe. We were packing our parachutes. Not much could calm my nerves now, but one calming thought was that I was going to jump with Cloudia again. I had given my parachute a name because it had saved my life so many times and I figured it was the least I could do to show my appreciation. She (the parachute was of course a female) was a Strato Cloud, manufactured in the United States. Cloudia and I had made 150 jumps together without any mishaps and I had the greatest respect for her. Bernard, on the other hand, had never before used his parachute. The former owner had made 900 jumps with the chute, which is considered a relatively high number for a parachute. Retirement age for a chute is about 1000 jumps. It can still be used, but will lose some of its performance, like a car with more than 150,000 miles.

Bernard had no idea how to pack a parachute for a BASE jump, and I admit I was clueless, too. We wanted the chute to open as quickly and dependably as possible. I thought for a while and came to the conclusion that the best way to pack it must be the "Skåne-packing." Bernard, of course, didn't understand the word itself, but I explained that it was the most popular way to pack parachutes in Skåne, Sweden. I watched Bernard as he happily packed his chute the "Skåne way." He knew I did not appreciate the fact that I, basically, was responsible for his packing. If something happened to Bernard, if his chute failed to deploy, I would feel guilty for the rest of my life.

In an attempt to cheer me up, he promised, "Jevto, don't worry! It's not such a big deal if I get killed. My parents will still have three living children."

After finishing Bernard's chute an hour later, I applied myself to packing Cloudia. I swept the ground to get rid of any small branches, leaves, and gravel. I carefully placed Cloudia on the cold asphalt. First, I checked that the suspension lines were not twisted. The I flattened every wrinkle and fold of the canopy. I then set the brakes, folded the canopy into the pack bag and closed the container. It is a strange feeling, packing your canopy in preparation for a BASE jump. When you dwell on the idea that your life depends on some nylon and a couple of lines, it can be a scary thought. I treated my canopy as if it were a newborn child. Every step in the packing was done with utmost care. One mistake, and…splat! I would be crushed against the ground at 80 mph. Thinking about the importance of my packing made me more than a little nervous. When I jump from airplanes, I deploy my canopy at 2000 feet, and if something should go wrong I still have all the time in the world to correct it. This was totally different. If something should happen when I jumped the 610-foot Kochertalbrücke, the prospects of fixing the problem were very small.

We were going to drive Bernard's tiny Renault 4 the 350 miles to our German friends in Frankfurt. The car didn't look like much with its rusty fenders and worn-out interior, but appearances can be deceptive. By now I had ridden in the little car many times in Paris and was impressed by its charm. To make the trip more comfortable, we designated three "Ministers," each responsible for a certain portfolio. Bernard was named Minister of Transportation, and was therefore responsible for driving. Scott was appointed Minister of Cartography and Music, in charge of finding our way and entertaining us with nice music during our trip. For this purpose, he recorded nine tapes with rock & roll music. Without any discussion whatsoever, I was selected Minister of Comestibles, so it was my duty to make sure there was enough food and drink in the car. We each contributed 500 francs which we put in a kitty for gas, tolls on the French highways, and food. The car was so heavily loaded that I almost felt sorry for it. Since it didn't have a roof-rack, everything was stowed in the trunk and under the seats.

As we left Paris on a hazy morning, I could feel a knot forming in my stomach. This was the point of no return. The adventure had begun. After 90 miles we arrived in Reims, which is famous for two things: its enormous Gothic cathedral and its champagne. Millions of bottles of champagne are produced every year in the Champagne region around Reims: Moët et Chandon, Veuve Cliquot,

Mumm, and Piper Heidsick, to mention just a few. We had beers in a café by the cathedral and then went inside. The cathedral was built between 1211-1427 and it's dimensions are impressive. It is more than 500 ft long and the height of the nave is 150 ft. A dozen candles burned peacefully inside and an elderly woman was on her knees on the cold stone floor, praying. I marveled at the patience involved in undertaking such an enormous project. A kind of patience all but forgotten in most of today's world.

Every block of stone had been pulled to the construction site and lifted by hand, one at a time. Strangely enough, many churches and cathedrals were spared from the bombs during the Second World War, while other nearby buildings fell like card houses. For the first time in my life, I lit a candle in a cathedral. I sat down on a wooden bench by the beautiful burning candles and prayed to whatever God who happened to be free for the day and had the time to listen.

"Dear God, whoever you are and wherever you are, please let our jumps from Kochertalbrücke be successful." With a calm heart I left the cathedral, just knowing we would be safe. Scott had brought his notebook and kept it within easy reach in the car. We made notations in it when we felt the urge. I put down my thoughts about the jump in a few lines. After another 30 miles we stopped in a small German town for dinner. We ordered a huge plate of sauerkraut and good German beer. Bernard watched with interest as the fat bartender spent five minutes skillfully filling our one-liter beer steins.

We arrived in Frankfurt at about one o'clock in the morning. Our German friends had been waiting for us for several hours and two of them had fallen asleep on the couch. With greetings and introductions out of the way, they showed us a video about BASE jumping. We watched the hour-long video with great interest: jumps from bridges, cliffs, cranes, buildings, antennas, every imaginable object. We scrutinized the bridge jumps, not wanting to miss a single detail. The film was produced and filmed by Carl Boenish. Often all it takes for a good dose of adrenaline to start flowing in my blood is watching the adventures of others. The BASE film gave me insomnia; sleep did not come to me until early morning. I was thinking about what I had seen on the screen and tried to instill the most important sequences in my brain. Tomorrow it was my turn to jump.

We awoke about ten in the morning and had a very filling German breakfast with our friends. According to the weather report, this was going to be a cloudy day with a temperature around 32° F. We learned that a film producer by the name of Klaus Heller was on his way from Munich with his entire film crew. Klaus owned a film company specializing in adventure films of various kinds. When he heard about our plans he became interested in shooting a film of our jumps. He had previous experience working with Carl Boenish in the United States, but so far didn't have any BASE footage of his own. We arranged to meet in the small village of Braunsbach, very close to the bridge.

In honor of the big day, Scott and I dressed in suits. I wore a navy double-breasted suit with a white shirt and red tie. Scott preferred a white shirt with black bow-tie. Our black shoes were shined to perfection. Bernard dressed in his usual way, jeans and a fisherman's sweater. Our German friends watched us change clothes and wondered if we had changed our minds about jumping. I told them, "Oh no. We just prefer to die in style."

This remark went completely over their heads. They didn't understand our sense of humor and took everything we said seriously. We were not transmitting on the same wavelength. After a three-hour drive, we arrived in Braunsbach and the Kochendörfer Inn, where Klaus and his film team were waiting. Klaus had brought along 45-year-old Rainer, who like Bernard and I, was planning to do his first BASE jump. He proudly showed us a photo he kept in his pocket. There he was, freefalling just above the treetops. Rainer explained he had agreed to deploy his canopy at the very latest moment for a film and estimated it had opened at 500 feet. This told us that he had three seconds left before impact at 120 mph. "This guy is one of the absolute craziest people in the world," I thought, not considering we might be just a little crazy ourselves, minutes away from jumping off a 610-foot-high bridge.

I could feel anxiety slowly but surely getting a grip on my body. At this point, there was no return, no way I dared tell the others, "Well, guys, I don't think I'll jump today." Actually, I think both Scott and Bernard felt the same way.

Klaus left us occasionally to check the light conditions outside and unfortunately, things did not look promising. A gray mist was in the air and it looked like it was going to rain. Klaus was disappointed after driving all the way from Munich to film us. If he returned without some action-filled footage, he would lose money after paying his staff. We waited in vain for more than two hours for the weather to improve. It was incredibly difficult to sit still and wait. We became more and more anxious and decided to jump despite the ugly weather. Thanking the innkeeper for her hospitality, we returned to the cars to get ready. I strapped on my parachute and pulled the leg straps tight. Tucking in my tie under the chest strap, I realized I had forgotten my tie clip. Disappointed, I envisioned the tie flopping around wildly during my freefall.

Scott prepared the drawing for the jump order. He jotted down a number on separate pieces of paper, one to four, and held out his hands. I crossed my fingers, hoping I would draw number one and be the first to jump. For some reason, I thought it would be less stressful if I could avoid watching the others jump before me. Bernard drew number three, Rainer one, Scott two, and I drew number four. I had to jump last. Next, we posed for the photographer. I must say we looked very sharp, not quite as you would expect for a bridge jump. Thirty minutes left before my jump and I could hear my own pulse raging inside my head, making it difficult to think clearly. Scott gave me a hard pat on the back, making me cough so hard I was afraid I'd cough up part of my insides. "It's time, Jevto. Keep your cool all the way down."

I smiled and nodded. Bernard had been very quiet the last half-hour, and I understood why. He was as nervous as I was. Even if Klaus and his team would not be able to film our jumps due to the weather, they were still interested in photographing us. Two photographers left before us to attach themselves to the bridge in specially made harnesses. This way they would be able to get first class photos of our exits. Time to go. The car ride from the valley up to the bridge took 15 minutes. We were boiling over from adrenaline and anxiety, resulting in energetic outbursts of yelling. Screaming is a good way to calm one's nerves. It may sound strange, but in situations where the body is under great psychological stress, a powerful scream can have a calming effect. I looked out through the car window and saw a sign announcing that we had a little more than three kilometers left to the jump site.

Scott played our favorite tape and turned up the volume. The singer in the group The Kinks yelled, "Catch me, I'm falling!" Our German driver, obviously lacking in humor, did not seem to appreciate the loud music. He had not uttered a single word since Braunsbach. Perhaps he was concentrating too hard. But then again, he was not going to jump, so we concluded he was simply a bore. I suddenly felt a tightness in my bladder. It was filled to the brim. I didn't want to ask the driver to pull over because I knew the police often patrolled the bridge to stop people from committing suicide. Since the construction of Kochertalbrücke, more than 50 people have jumped to their deaths, without parachutes. At the same time, I certainly didn't want to do my first BASE jump with a full bladder. There was only one solution: relax where I was sitting in the backseat and let nature take its course. I informed Scott of my plan and he started to laugh. He waved his hand and yelled a warning directed to Bernard. Afterwards Scott told our driver what I had just done in the backseat of his nice Mercedes. He turned around and confirmed the catastrophe and addressed me with some very naughty words. I figured I had made an enemy for life, but luckily I would never see him again.

We arrived on the bridge and I felt my heart beat a couple extra times from fear. In only minutes I would begin a fantastic adventure, a trip into the world of extreme feelings and excitement. As a 12-year-old, I had earned the world record for standing on one foot without support. I stood on my right foot for 5 hours and 46 minutes in front of several witnesses. The editor of the Guinness Book of World Records, Norris McWhirter, confirmed my world record and informed me it would be included in the next edition of the record book. Unfortunately my record was broken by an American before the book was published. At that time, I considered my record a fantastic adventure. This was a totally different adventure, something psychologists call "self-inflicted highly dangerous behavior."

The car pulled to the side and stopped. I walked to the railing to check the view. The valley below was shrouded in mist and fog. Bernard chose not to look down, explaining it would only frighten him. The photographers were ready in their harnesses below the bridge. Bernard attached our static lines to the bridge railing and I asked him to check and recheck that they were firmly anchored. The static line was 15 feet long and terminated with a break cord attached to the pilot chute. When I jumped, the static line would stretch, pulling out the chute until the break cord would snap, allowing the canopy to deploy fully.

One by one, we climbed over the railing. The ledge was only four inches wide and I hung on to the railing with one hand. Rainer, who was going to jump first, was concentrating. I could see his breath against the gray sky, then it suddenly stopped. A mysterious quiet fell over the bridge. I was unconsciously holding my breath as Rainer graciously leapt off the bridge into the inhospitable air. He made a three-second freefall, then his canopy opened with a bang. We could hear him yell in excitement as he realized he had successfully made it through the first part of the jump. A short while later, one of us had landed safely on the field below the bridge. As I hung on to the railing, cars were rushing past at high speed. I don't think the passengers had time to notice what was happening in front of them. But if somebody caught sight of the four of us jumping from the bridge they would have a hard time convincing friends and family about what they saw: "Look! There's a man in a suit and tie jumping from the bridge"

Scott's turn was up. He checked his equipment one last time. Everything seemed to be in order. He wanted to make a good exit and took great care in positioning his feet against the edge of the bridge. He composed himself by turning his face toward the dark gray sky one more time. Yelling something incomprehensible, he took a mighty leap. Bernard and I could hear him screaming all the way down until his canopy opened. A few seconds later, he landed next to

Rainer on the snow-covered field. Rainer and Scott stood unharmed on the field below, happy to be alive. Bernard and I still had a decision to make. Did we dare jump? Was I going to climb back over the bridge railing at the last minute? As these thoughts went through my mind, Bernard took up his position on the exit ramp. Poor Bernard. I could feel his nervousness. With bad luck, he could be dead before he could count to ten. Bernard managed a weak smile, pushed himself off the bridge with great strength, leaving me alone on top of the bridge. Sure, the photographers were hanging in their harnesses close by, but as far as I was concerned, they belonged to an entirely different world. I heard Bernard's screams of joy below his blue parachute. I was relieved his chute had opened like it should.

I was alone. I had never before felt so alone. Semi trucks roared by only ten feet away, but I didn't hear them. My brain was blocked to any inessential information. I am not sure I would have reacted even if a hand grenade had exploded close by. Suddenly, I felt calm and it surprised me. I tried to find a good place for my feet. There. I looked to the sky and locked my eyes on a big gray cloud, preparing for a good exit. My position was good, my feet steady. An impulse from my brain reached my legs and I instinctively pushed off. I was met by a wonderful quietness, which turned into a soft buzz as I fell. Looking down toward the ground, I was shocked to see it come rushing toward me with terrible speed. Swoosh! I was hanging below my beloved Cloudia. My brain was in turmoil as the adrenaline flowed through my system.

We made it. I brought Cloudia to a standstill 3 feet above the ground and landed softly as if on a bed of cotton. Cloudia was on top of me as I rolled around, ecstatic. Scott came running toward me with something in his hand. Before I knew what hit me, he had smeared my face with mud. My face black with mud, I stood on my knees and yelled to nobody in particular. I needed to rid my body of some of the extra energy bubbling inside me.

Uwe of the film team let his camera sweep across the joyful scene played out before him. For the first time I realized what the expression *walking on air* really meant. I had no sensation of the ground under my feet. Bernard was just as exhilarated as I was. He bounced around for joy in the field like a young buck. Scott, Bernard, and I hugged each other with all our might. In my capacity as Minister of Comestibles, I had brought a bottle of champagne which we opened to celebrate our accomplishments. With the bottle in one hand and Cloudia in the other I squeezed into Klaus' minivan. We took off for the small inn in Braunsbach where we had been contemplating our jumps earlier. Rainer was singing in the back seat. Scott was drinking champagne and letting out cries of joy, "Yahoo! Yeah! Yippee!"

Bernard sat quietly by himself, whispering, *"Ce n'est pas vrai…ce n'est pas vrai. Quel pied!"* (No way…no way! Incredible!)

I had jumped from a 610-foot-high bridge and I was still alive. My arms were intact, my legs, too. I was happy in an uncomplicated way. The inn was already in full swing when we arrived. The bar, which normally served about ten customers a day, was suddenly invaded by a loud, obnoxious group. The evening would be most memorable. Rainer ordered a round of beer and good French cognac for the whole gang. I sat down by Bernard and Scott. We looked each other in the eyes and cheered for our first success. A helpful older German gentleman decided to clean my face and removed the mud from my cheeks and neck with a wet rag. There was a definite shortage of women. Actually, there was only one. Her name was Gertrud and she owned the place. She was blond with an impressive bust and must have weighed just over 220 pounds. Scott noticed she kept a close eye on me, and advised me to watch out.

Bernard had just accomplished his 71st jump. For someone who had difficulty controlling his body in freefall, a BASE jump was a tremendous accomplishment. I had spent three months mulling over whether to jump or not, and it was clear that if it had not been for Scott, I would never have made a BASE jump. Bernard had made his decision in a minute. We had known each other for just short of two months, but despite the short time we felt very close. People who experience dangerous situations together often become very close. Consider special forces teams, expeditions under difficult physical conditions, or castaways floating around on a raft. There is no doubt that those who have been close to death and survived have a different outlook on life.

Also, when you have experienced the feeling of adrenaline flowing through your body, you always come back for more. You consciously put yourself in similar dangerous situations. It becomes a drug. Just think about the war photographers who time and time again go into life-threatening situations. Nobody forces them to do it. They make their own decisions. Of course the purpose is ostensibly to take great photos, but mostly it's to experience a good dose of adrenaline. Like all drugs, adrenaline produces a high and a low. It gives a feeling of euphoria, happiness, strength, speed, total well-being. The high may last from a minute to several hours. Then, the down period sets in, with fatigue and drowsiness. That's all it is. The body is totally spent from being in a state of high stress and needs to relax and recharge its batteries. It is best to run all systems on low for a while and the brain will see to it that sleep sets in.

Back in Frankfurt we were definitely in the down period, so we hit the sack. I slept till just before lunch the following day without moving even an inch. When I awoke, I felt alert and full of energy. I had accomplished what I came for and looked forward to a pleasant trip back to Paris. If only Scott had been as reasonable. He wanted to go back to Kochertalbrücke, 155 miles away, for one more jump. He insisted we must not miss the opportunity for another jump as long as there was a nice bridge in the neighborhood. He was not going back to Paris without making a second BASE jump. My first reaction was intense: no way was I going to jump again. We had all made our jumps and that was enough. I did not feel like going through the preparations, the anxiety, the tension, and the fear again. As I was arguing fiercely, I suddenly realized Scott was right. The only reason I refused another jump was fear. I knew how nervous I would be and it was only natural to react the way I did and say, "Okay. That's done. Let's go home."

Often it takes even more courage to return to the fire a second time. Scott insisted, and after a while he had talked me into it. Bernard remained quiet during our heated discussion. We convinced the Germans to make another trip. I left my muddy suit in the trunk of the car this time.

A Brush with Death

We arrived in Braunsbach about 3 p.m. Two of the Germans also wanted to jump, so there were five of us. They drove straight to the bridge while we drove down into the valley. We were planning to photograph their jumps from below and it is always a good idea to have someone waiting at the landing site in case of injuries. We agreed that they would wave their arms when they were ready to jump. With the help of binoculars we could follow everything that happened up on the bridge. We waited until the time we had agreed upon, but no jumpers appeared on the bridge or came falling down. Bernard speculated that they had been overcome by fear and turned around.

Suddenly, a car came speeding toward us. It was the Germans. It came to an abrupt halt a few feet in front of us, and they jumped out of the car and yelled that the police were after them. I looked down the road but didn't see any police cars. They yelled and hollered and waved their arms as if an entire division of enemy tanks were after them. We tried in vain to calm them down. They got in the car and hid it behind a grove of trees. After they calmed down a little, the Germans told us what had happened. A police car had stopped on the bridge, and they had been ordered to open the trunk where the officers found the parachutes. Our guess was that someone from the village who had watched us jump the day before had tipped off the police. The Germans got a stern warning from the officers and were told to be on their way immediately. The officers had succeeded in frightening the Germans enough to make them believe they were being followed. Their only wish now was to return to Frankfurt.

Scott, Bernard, and I still wanted to jump. We figured we hadn't driven 155 miles just to be chased away by some police officers we hadn't even seen. The only problem was that we needed the Germans' help to drive us onto the bridge. They refused, explaining they would probably end up in jail and lose their driver's licenses if they got caught. Scott was furious and raised his voice while I, with typical Nordic calm, tried to talk them down. One of the Germans finally agreed to drive us to the jump site on the bridge, but made it clear that he would leave as soon as he dropped us off.

A beautiful full moon brightened the winter night, which would otherwise have been pitch-black. Bernard and I prepared ourselves for our first manual BASE jumps. This time, we were going to freefall instead of using the static line. It was our first night jump. Someone, I don't remember who, got the excellent idea that we should all jump at the same time. Bernard would be in the middle with Scott and myself on each side. On a given signal, the three of us would take the leap together. It was also the first time we were to use what was to become our battle cry, *Je suis le plus bête* (freely translated: I am the biggest idiot). We felt it was an appropriate battle cry for what we were up to.

I had instructed the driver to drop us off by the marker 680.5, which indicated the middle of the bridge and was also the highest point above the valley. We reached the point in about 15 minutes and strangely enough, I felt less nervous this time. The driver dropped us off and took off at high speed. I resolutely walked up to the railing and climbed over, holding my pilot chute in one hand and hanging on to the railing with the other. For some reason I looked down and what I saw shocked me. I thought I saw pine trees swaying in the wind about 200 feet below. Without a word, I looked down again and realized my eyes had seen correctly. I was on a four-inch-wide ledge 200 feet above ground, hanging on for life with one hand. We had the wrong spot. I was terrified and hardly dared move. If I fell, it would be toward a certain death. Scott, who still had not climbed the railing, grabbed my arm and pulled me to safety. We searched for the correct marker and found it a fair distance away. I walked up to the marker and read the numbers, 680.5, to make sure we were in the right place this time. The driver had dropped us off 1,600 feet too soon, which could have cost us all our lives. I didn't dare think of the newspaper headlines if we had jumped in good faith from the bridge to be crushed on impact 200 feet below. I climbed the railing again and positioned myself on the narrow ledge. Bernard was 50 feet to my right and Scott was another fifty feet further. Bernard had been designated to give the all-clear and asked me if I was ready. "Yes," I answered, loud and clear.

He turned to Scott and posed the same question. "Yes," Scott answered. As Bernard gave me a final glance, we heard Scott yell, "No! I'm not ready. Wait!"

I couldn't tell what was wrong because Bernard was in the way, but I knew something serious must have happened. Bernard climbed back over the railing and walked over to Scott. They monkeyed around with his rig for a few minutes, then the countdown started over. We counted together, "Three! Two! One!" The three of us jumped at the exact same time, yelling, *"Je suis le plus bête!"*

I fell for three seconds and then released Mr. Black, my pilot chute. Cloudia opened perfectly, always faithful, and I tried to get my bearings as quickly as possible. I could barely see the ground despite the moonlight and I hoped I wouldn't have the misfortune of landing with one foot in a rabbit hole. Hanging under my canopy I attempted to locate Bernard's and Scott's canopies, but it was too dark. At 165 feet, I discovered I was just above the river which runs through the valley, and corrected my position with the help of the steering toggles. I made a soft landing in the frostbitten grass. My first concern after landing was to find Bernard and Scott. I yelled at the top of my lungs, "Bernard! Scott!"

No answer! I started to worry. Were they in trouble? I called their names several times and was finally relieved to hear Bernard's voice reply, "Here! I landed by the river!"

I ran up to him and we hugged. But we could not declare our jumps successful until Scott had been found. His chances of making it were slim if he had landed in the river. A wet canopy is very heavy and tends to push the jumper down under the water. We walked back and forth along the river without finding a trace of Scott or his canopy. Perhaps he landed on the other side of the river? We were about to cross the river on a tiny bridge downstream when Scott appeared. He came walking calmly along the road with the canopy in his arms. We ran up to him and asked what had happened. He told us he had landed on the other side of the river and had not been able to cross it until he found the tiny bridge.

I took the opportunity to ask Scott why he had climbed back over the railing just as we were about to jump. He solemnly told me he had never been as close to death as at that moment. As Bernard began the countdown, Scott noticed he had accidentally fastened the bridle cord, the line between the pilot chute and main canopy, under his leg strap. Had he jumped, the canopy would never have deployed. He would have been history. This taught us all something very important: always let your personal safety come first. This may sound elementary, but it is easy to be influenced by other factors in the surroundings. Instead of brushing off the Germans' story about the police, we had unconsciously been affected by it, and so we had decided to put on our rigs in the car. This is how Scott made his mistake. We promised each other to use the US Marine's philosophy in the future: K.I.S.S. (Keep It Simple Stupid). In difficult and stressful situations, everything runs smoother if you don't complicate things. The Germans were jealous and didn't even mention our jumps. We thanked them, in a somewhat ironic tone, for all their help and left on our long journey to Paris.

That Crazy Swede

It was good to be back in Paris. I felt safe sleeping in my own bed, knowing I would not be jumping from a bridge in the morning. The world around me was reassuring and comfortable. The first week after our return, I told my closest friends about our adventure. I soon found people always asked me the same questions: "Where do you get the guts to jump off a bridge? What happens if the canopy doesn't open?"

At first, I gladly answered these questions, but after a while it became tiring and I found myself making up answers along the lines of MAD's "Smart comebacks to stupid questions" to avoid further discussions. When my co-workers at Facit heard what I had done, they shook their heads and called me *le suédois fou* (the crazy Swede), which I took as a compliment. I thought long and hard whether I should tell my family about my jump, but decided it was too soon.

My daily life in Paris was entertaining but hectic. I got up at seven in order to be at work by nine. I would skip breakfast so I could take a shower or a bath. Due to the location of my bathtub, my room would always be dripping wet afterwards.

The layout of my small room proved a fantastic opportunity for striking it up with beautiful young *au pair* girls. After having spent the whole week cleaning, ironing, cooking, and taking care of somebody else's screaming kids, they would be fed up. I sat in my room one evening, sipping from a bottle of single Malt, and strategizing. "How can I use this to my advantage?" I wondered. I started going to bars where a lot of Swedish, Norwegian, Danish, and Dutch *au pairs* hung out. Very quickly I realized that a lot of them were longing for a good, hot bubble bath in a nice, romantic environment. One night I offered a Danish *au pair* the chance to use the bathtub in my apartment whenever she wanted to. I didn't explain that my apartment was only 100 square feet and that the bathtub was in the middle of the room. Needless to say there wasn't any privacy at all. A couple of days later she knocked on the door, and as soon as she entered the room I could see that she was a bit surprised. She looked at me with a smile, asked me to draw the bath, and got ready. I sat quietly on my bed reading a book while she took her bath, and the rest is history. This little trick didn't always work though, and on more than one occasion they stalked out of the room swearing in their native language.

My workday began with a sack-full of mail which I emptied on the desk. I opened and sorted each piece of mail according to department: IT, sales, human resources, and administration. It was a routine job which took me about an hour. After sorting the mail, I could take my first break of the day. I went downstairs to the basement where one of my good friends in the company, Colette, worked. She was what I call a "dish lady." Her job was to dish up the food in the personnel dining room, located in the dark basement. She liked me, which showed in the huge sandwiches she prepared for me. Colette would take a break when I came downstairs, and we usually engaged in conversation about her favorite topic, the Lottery. She gambled away hundreds of francs every week and she was absolutely certain she would eventually win millions. In the name of good manners, I tried my best to seem interested when she explained her various systems and calculations that would make her win big. I spent a large amount of my working hours sending telex messages, drawing up sales diagrams, and translating. Working for Ylva Berthelson, who had an important role in the company, I gained many insights into how a medium-sized company is run. At lunchtime, all activity within the company ceased for an hour and a half. In the employee dining room, we had a choice of three appetizers, three entrees, and cheese or dessert. Most employees would have a carafe of red wine with lunch. After lunch, work resumed, continuing till six in the evening.

Once or twice a week, employees organized what the French call a *pot*. When someone had something to celebrate, he or she invited everybody to one or several drinks in the employee dining room. Notices were posted in hallways a few days before the *pot* to make sure as many people as possible would show up. A *pot* could be held for a variety of reasons: childbirth, retirement, marriage, etc. The reasons for a *pot* were limited only by one's imagination. A *pot* usually lasted for about an hour and the most common drinks were champagne and whisky. The human resource department discussed what could be done to limit the number of celebrations, as they naturally had a negative effect on productivity. I always had plenty of time and participated in every *pot*.

One evening, Bernard and a friend, a geology student, organized a party in the catacombs of Paris. Scott and I were told we were going to spend the night in the catacombs with about twenty geologists. He asked us to bring wine, cheese and bread as well as a good party-mood. What were the catacombs, really? I knew about the catacombs of Rome from school. I also knew that it was possible for tourists to visit the Paris catacombs, but I had no idea it was possible to party a whole night in the tunnels below the city. We had agreed to meet close to the Denfert Rochereau subway station early Friday evening. Everybody was told to bring candles and a hard-hat. Without a hard-hat the top of our heads would be scraped up badly against the low ceilings. It sounded like an adventure.

Scott, Bernard, and I prepared our food packages together. Scott had baked brownies and I had prepared pea soup as it is done in Skåne. We bet a case of beer for the first person who found a skeleton in the catacombs. Gathering at the meeting place, I was just a little disappointed about the few women that were present; only six of the twenty partygoers were women. Our leader and guide, Jean-Jacques, wore a bright gas lamp on his helmet so he wouldn't lead us astray in the maze below ground. He also had a map of Paris underground, without which our party would have been impossible. Spotting me among the guests, he laughed and informed me that my stature, 6 ft. 6 in., was not ideal for a visit to the catacombs.

I was the last guest to crawl into the narrow tunnel. After crawling about ten feet, I stood up and lit my candle. I was prepared for the worst. The first thing I noticed was the year 1803 inscribed in the wall in front of me. I racked my brain for historical facts but was unable to connect 1803 with any event of importance. The destination this evening was a large cave which Jean-Jacques had discovered during an earlier tour. The flame from my candle lit up the rough stone walls as I advanced through the darkness. In my youth the ghost-train ride at the Tivoli Gardens in Copenhagen was one of my absolute favorites. Walking through the narrow tunnels below Paris, I was thankful for this previous experience in the world of horror. The atmosphere was creepy to say the least. Every so often Jean-Jacques stopped to take a bearing with his compass. I will never understand how he managed to find his way through the maze of tunnels. Sometimes we passed cave-like openings, where we could see limestone deposits up to five feet high. On our way to the party-room, we stopped at two of these openings to wash down the dust in our throats with a gulp of cold beer. Once, during our walk, my candle died and I lost contact with the rest of the group. If Scott hadn't noticed I was missing, I would probably still be below Paris today. The French woman ahead of me announced we had five more minutes of stumbling until we reached the party-cave. I was very happy to hear this because my back was sending me frequent messages of complaints. No wonder; I had been in a crouched position for more than two hours.

We finally reached our destination. The cave was 60 feet long and 30 feet wide. The walls were rough and covered with artistic reproductions of skeletons in phosphorescent colors. This particular cave was commonly used by geology students in Paris to celebrate the end of long final exams. One of the French women placed a candle in the cave, another retrieved the food from our backpacks. I began serving my homemade pea soup from Skåne and at the same time offered each guest a glass of cold punch, a sweet Swedish liqueur. The first protests came as I was explaining the history of *ärtsoppa*, the pea soup traditionally served every Thursday in the province of Skåne.

"Yuck! What is this disgusting glop?"

The pea soup was a total flop. The French did not appreciate my Swedish cooking and I had to finish two liters of pea soup by myself. I should have given them *surströmming* (sour fermented herring) instead, I thought viciously. We sat on the floor in a circle, listening to Haendel, eating and drinking. After the dinner, we danced in the surrounding galleries. The French refused to dance to any other music than classic rock-n-roll from the Fifties, even in the catacombs.

We partied till late that night below the city of Paris and it was around three in the morning when we finally began to make our way back to the surface. I had no idea where we were going, but it certainly seemed like a long way. Three hours later, I was the first to climb up the 60-foot ladder, which according to Jean-Jacques led to a metal cover on a sidewalk in downtown Paris. I had been instructed to wait on top of the ladder until everybody was in position before I pushed open the heavy cover. This was necessary in order to make a quick and discreet exit. The cover proved to be heavier than expected, and I had to ask my colleague below me for help. We pushed for all we were worth and finally managed to slide it over enough to squeeze through. Things looked peaceful and quiet above ground.

I returned to the land of the living, closely followed by my friend, the cover-lifter. Once we were standing on the sidewalk, I spotted a police van 150 feet away. I immediately notified the others, who still had one leg in the grave, of the approaching danger. My friend above ground suggested that we run and unfortunately I agreed. We took off and ran for all we were worth. It wasn't long before we heard the characteristic siren, followed by screeching tires. The police car skidded around a street corner like Starsky and Hutch, blocking our escape. Four muscular policemen jumped out of the car. They wanted to know what we had been up to underground and I answered I was just coming home from a party. My answer was waved off as a bad lie. After more than five minutes on the ladder, Jean-Jacques and the rest of the gang decided to climb through the hole onto the sidewalk. They had heard the police siren and were just a little nervous. Unbelievably, they chose to run toward us instead of away; I almost lost it when they appeared, sprinting as fast as they could. By this time, I was handcuffed to a police officer. One of the policemen pulled his revolver, a .357 Smith & Wesson, at the sight of eighteen people charging toward him. This made everybody stop in their tracks. Bernard, the front-runner, lifted his arms above his head, signaling that he gave himself up. They were body searched and subjected to a short interrogation. The chief, a man about fifty, thought we were telling the truth, and our only punishment was replacing the cover and a warning to stay away from the catacombs.

Later, I found out why the police had reacted so fiercely. We happened to emerge through a hole in the street at six in the morning, exactly in front of Société Génerale, one of the biggest banks in Paris. Besides, we were all carrying small backpacks. In the early 80s, a gang in Lyon robbed a big bank of everything deposited in the bank vault. They entered the bank one Saturday evening by drilling a hole from the underground. Before they disappeared, they celebrated with cheese, bread, and wine. The end of our party had been exciting, but the weapon in the policeman's hand had scared me. French policemen are at least as trigger-happy as their American colleagues. A while later, I made a point of reading a few books about the catacombs in Paris and learned some interesting facts. The catacombs did not initially serve as a graveyard; they were originally quarries used for the construction of many of the city's beautiful sandstone buildings. In 1871, it was decided by the police chief of Paris that the old bones of the city's overflowing cemeteries should be removed. All the old skeletons were thrown into the excavations below ground. This is how Paris underground became a burial ground.

Home of the Gods

Shortly after our return to Paris, we began planning for our next BASE jump. The site was decided upon unanimously: the Montparnasse Tower. Scott had already tumbled once jumping from the building and we felt it was a good idea to make use of his near-death experience. Montparnasse Tower was built during the Presidency of Georges Pompidou. The building is 56 stories high and constructed of concrete and glass. Its name is derived from Greek mythology, in which Mount Parnassus is the home of Apollo, the sun god. A restaurant and bar are located on the 56th floor; it's a popular tourist spot because of the amazing view, which only Eiffel Tower is able to beat.

On a beautiful Sunday afternoon in early March 1984, we took the elevator to the observation deck to get a closer look at the jump site. We wanted to inspect the tall fence, erected to serve as a deterrent to suicide. The elevator is extremely fast: 40 seconds to the top of the 693-foot-tall building. The first thing we noticed was a couple of uniformed guards checking our tickets as we stepped out of the elevator. According to Scott, if we could get past them with our parachutes, the coast was clear until we reached the observation deck. The guards' normal pattern was two rounds of the deck each hour for the purpose of stopping people from committing suicide. They say that over 200 people have jumped to their deaths from Montparnasse Tower.

Scott pointed out the spot from where he made his first jump from the building. The suicide fence would be difficult to ignore. It measured eight feet, topped with four inches of sharp spikes. We would have to use a rope to climb the fence safely. The tourist season was approaching and the deck would be crowded with curious tourists at the time of our jump. For a short while, we entertained the idea of making some money by selling tickets to anyone interested in watching us. Scott jokingly suggested we make a deal with the Tower management and jump twice a day during tourist season. "Watch three typical Parisians jump from skyscraper, every day at noon—100 francs." We returned to the deck three more times over the next two weeks. On one of the visits, we brought a big suitcase to study the guards' reaction. We planned to pack the three parachutes in the suitcase and sneak them on deck. The guards reaction was exactly what we had hoped for: nonexistent.

Bernard, Scott, and I spent many evenings planning our jumps. We came to the conclusion that it would indeed look suspicious if three guys each brought a suitcase and therefore we worked out a detailed plan of action. (We had already forgotten the promise we made each other in Braunsbach to "Keep It Simple Stupid," and we were to suffer for it again.) Scott was to dress like an American tourist in big, baggy jeans and an unshapely T-shirt, backpack, and the mandatory camera on his chest. Bernard didn't have to change outfits. He was to resemble a French student and could keep his usual clothes: jeans, leather jacket, and sneakers. My own disguise would be as a young businessman: dark suit, white shirt, striped tie, and shiny black shoes. Who would suspect a well-dressed young man of wanting to throw himself from a building? Nobody.

The disguises were part of our psychological preparations for the jump and helped a little in calming our nerves. It gave us something else to think about besides the guards and the jump itself. Each of us was also going to contact a young woman to accompany us as a diversion in case we were discovered by the guards. If that happened, the women would charm the guards while we jumped. It was up to each girl how far she wanted to take this game. They were also supposed to pick up the rope which we would leave on the deck.

Possible escape plans were also discussed in detail. Scott suggested arranging for a getaway car at the foot of the building, but was voted down. We felt it would be too cumbersome for three people with parachutes to get into a car quickly, especially if we were being chased. The subway seemed to be our best bet. If we jumped at around six in the evening, the subway would be packed with commuters and we could easily disappear in the crowd. In case we got arrested after the jump, the only consequence would be a fine. France does not have a law prohibiting jumps from buildings and it is not forbidden to commit suicide by jumping from the Montparnasse Tower. On the other hand, climbing over the fence on the deck *is* against the law. We felt that the risk of having to pay a fine was worth taking.

I looked at the Tower differently now than six months earlier. What had once been an anonymous high-rise was now a frightening creature I had to defeat. Each time I glanced up toward the deck, I seemed to hear the building grumbling. "You little whippersnapper! Jump from my deck and it'll be the last thing you do. You may think you'll make it in one piece, but you just wait and see. I'll make sure you never see the light of day again."

My defensive weapon was getting to know my opponent as well as possible. I visited the deck twice more without Scott and Bernard. This was extremely important to me. I needed to experience the fear on my own. There is a big difference between being afraid in the company of good friends and being afraid alone. In a group, constant pep talks keep the morale and confidence up; alone, you have only yourself for encouragement. Standing on the deck I realized what an exciting show we were about to put on for the tourists who had come to admire the view. The 18 francs they paid for a ticket would also give them the opportunity to see three young men leap from the edge of the roof 693 feet above ground. A very reasonable price to pay for such excitement.

In the middle of our preparations, the subject of discussion turned to plastic bags. Bernard and I did not own a backpack like Scott's, and we now felt it would be too cumbersome to carry large suitcases onto the deck. We needed something lightweight and convenient in which to hide our parachutes. Bernard mentioned plastic bags and we started searching for something suitable. It was not an easy task to find a plastic bag big enough to hold a parachute. One day, Scott called me at work and told me he had found the perfect plastic bag, a Fnac bag. Fnac is a French department store chain that sells records, books, and camera equipment. The bag was rectangular and made of heavy plastic with two sturdy handles. I went to Fnac and purchased four of the bags in case one of them broke during the trials.

Each time we met in Scott's apartment for a planning session, it felt like we were planning a terrorist attack. We talked about how to get past the guards, who would attach the rope for climbing over the fence, and how we would react in case we were discovered. I think that's what made our planning so exciting. There was only about a week left before jump day. I contacted Arin, a Mexican-American girl I had met in a bar, and asked her to help. After I explained her part in the adventure, she willingly agreed to make sure the guards did not stop us from jumping. According to Arin herself, she was an accomplished photographer which suited us fine as we would very much like to have some photos of the jumps. Scott asked two girls from Lund, Maria and Helena, to assist him and Bernard. We asked them to be at the Tower entrance at 5:30 in the evening, March 22.

One of the few things yet to be dealt with was the dreadful lottery for jump order. It was going to take place at Scott's, where we also planned to enjoy a nice supper. One week until the jump, and I was already nervous. Something unreal was slowly becoming a reality. The Tower frightened me. Did I really want to jump from a building in downtown Paris? What if I got hit by a car when I landed, or what if I crashed through a window on my way down? Because Scott had already jumped from the Tower, we would be drawing the numbers two, three, and four.

We opened a bottle of Jack Daniels and placed it on the table in front of us. I poured a glass for each of us while Scott prepared for the drawing. I hoped with all my heart that I would not draw the number 4 and have to jump last from the deck. It is one thing to jump from a bridge surrounded by greenery in a calm and quiet atmosphere and another thing to stand all alone on a roof in downtown Paris waiting for your turn. Scott put the pieces of paper in a bowl and mixed them up. We each pulled one out and I hurriedly opened mine.

"I jump as number two," said Scott.

I opened my piece of paper and saw the number 4. I was terribly disappointed. I would have to jump last again. Bernard was first. Neither Bernard nor Scott could keep from laughing when they realized I had lost again.

"This is not funny!" I yelled. "Once is okay, but not twice in a row. I think one of you should switch places with me." It was not going to be that easy. Bernard was happy to be the first off the roof and refused to switch. Scott was definitely not going to jump last and commented, "Jevto, you're getting used to jumping last so you might as well continue to be last. You could get real good at it some day."

I calmed down eventually and enjoyed the delicious dinner Scott had prepared. We spent the rest of the evening in a bar, listening to an American blues band. Conversation was about anything except the jump. It felt good to be able to relax and give the brain a break.

We had planned to pack our chutes in the market place outside Scott's apartment, as we did before the Kochertalbrücke jump. The market was open for business every Thursday and Saturday morning. Several pot-bellied men arrived in the afternoon the day before to erect the six and-a-half foot tall metal poles quickly and with precision. The poles were then covered with tarpaulins to protect the merchandise from rain and sun. When business was over about two in the afternoon, the same group of muscular men returned and removed the poles.

I am crazy about avocados. A young man from California sold the biggest and best avocados I have ever tasted. I also made a habit of stopping by the fish-stand to buy a dozen oysters to eat for lunch. With every oyster lunch, my mood improved as I tasted the freshness of the ocean. I seldom purchased meat as I didn't have a refrigerator to store it in.

We packed our chutes on Saturday afternoon after the market closed. Cloudia was spread out again on the hard asphalt. I could tell that she was excited that she would be flying again soon. We had figured out that it took a stone seven seconds to fall from the top of the Tower to the ground 693 feet below. We would spend four of these seven seconds in free fall, leaving three seconds to impact. Not a big window of opportunity. It is scary to do something which can affect your life to such a degree that there is absolutely no time for a mistake: seven ridiculously short seconds between life and death.

The Montparnasse Tower towered over us as we packed our chutes. I looked up at the building, a mile southwest of the market place and said, "You'll see, you little building; I'm gonna beat you! You don't stand a chance."

The beautiful and majestic Eiffel Tower watched us from the north. We had thought about jumping from the Eiffel Tower, but had come to the conclusion that the Montparnasse Tower was a better object for BASE jumps. The Eiffel Tower is cone-shaped. Without a truly exceptional exit, it would be difficult to avoid the steel beams during freefall, a prospect that did not appeal to us. I don't mean to argue that there is no risk in jumping from the Montparnasse Tower. There is always the risk of crushing every bone in your body. It is a question of weighing the risks against each other and selecting the least dangerous.

Finished packing, we each went home to our own apartments. None of us slept well that night. Bernard was awake half the night wondering if he should prepare a will. Scott thought about what he would do in the event that one of us should die. I was thinking that if this was my time to die, I would prefer to die quickly. It is a strange phenomenon, the distance one feels from death when something very dangerous is about to happen. My reasoning was calm, concrete, and cold as I thought about something most people are afraid of: death. Putting myself in these types of situations, I had thought about death more times than I could count. Sometimes, the thoughts would stay with me for days. It was all very tiring.

On D-Day, I got out of bed at seven as usual to go to work. I was not very productive that day. Ylva Berthelson wondered if I felt sick, but I could not tell her the real reason for my poor performance. She would find out the following day. I did not accomplish a single significant thing during my eight hours in the office. After a few minutes of trying to figure out the week's sales of computers, my thoughts would drift to the jump.

A young man from Cambodia, Rainsy, noticed my unusually contemplative mood. Rainy was responsible for the mail at Facit. He was a small man, very thin and dark-skinned. During the Vietnam War, he flew DC-3s for the American Air

Force with the job of transporting weapons to the front. He was shot down three times, but always recovered remarkably from his serious injuries. Rainsy often talked about the DC-3, an aircraft he still admired. When his parents were murdered by the Khmer Rouge in 1975, Rainsy escaped with his wife to France via Thailand. Rainsy and I often talked. I told him about skydiving and he told me about his combat experiences as a pilot. We respected each other and got along great. I imagine we both had a fondness for adventure. Rainsy was the only person who knew we were going to jump from the Tower. I invited him to come and watch.

Shortly after lunch, I cleaned off my desk and left for home. Cloudia was ready, waiting for me on my bed. I was sure she could sense what was about to happen. I sat down by my desk to write a note to I didn't know who. I took a letter-sized white paper and wrote:

> "I have gone to jump off the Montparnasse Tower. I am making this jump of my own free will and only because I think it is exciting and fun."

If, for some reason, I didn't survive the jump, I did not want my parents and friends to have any doubt about my true intentions.

Bernard had already arrived at Scott's apartment when I walked in. He appeared to be in good shape psychologically. Neither Scott nor Bernard appeared nervous, but I suspected that on the inside they were just as anxious as I was. I asked Scott for some black shoe polish to touch up my shoes as they had lost their shine. After all, it's very important to have shiny shoes when jumping off tall buildings.

Trollveggen and the launch site Bruraskaret.
Photo, Knut Aune Kunstforlag.

Our two norwegian guides, Ronald and Svein, rest with Bernard
on our way up to Trollveggen (Notice the warning sign).
Photo, Jevto Dedijer.

Bernard seconds before he nearly strikes the cliff in freefall.
Photo, Ronald Ytterli.

Bernard takes off and leaves me alone on the top of a wind struck cliff.
Photo, Ronald Ytterli.

The point of no return. One minute after having thrown up,
I jump from the 2000ft Trollveggen.
Photo, Ronald Ytterli.

I connect with the Gods. Photo, Scott Elder.

I leap of the 610ft Kochertalbrücke with a borrowed parachute (bad idea!).
Photo, Scott Elder.

Kochertalbrücke shrouded in fog and mist. Photo, Klaus Heller.

Beautiful Braunsbach in Germany. Photo, U. Zink.

Bernard strolling along the Rauma river the day after our jumps from
Trollveggen. Life is good.
Photo, Jevto Dedijer.

The 876ft New River Gorge Bridge in West Virginia.
Photo, Jürgen Lorenzen.

A crowd of 100,000 watch Scott concentrate seconds before he leaps
from the 876ft New River bridge. Photo, Bernard Poirier.

Scott does it perfectly. Photo, Bernard Poirier.

Bernard makes a bad exit from New River bridge.
A second later he is falling head down. Photo, Scott Elder.

Bernard having fun. Photo, Jevto Dedijer.

Scott's first BASE jump wearing a tuxedo.
Photo, Klaus Heller.

Dressed for action. The three of us minutes before our first jump from 650ft. Kochertalbrücke. Photo, Klaus Heller.

The joy of feeling fully alive. Photo, Klaus Heller.

Celebrating our first BASE jump together. Photo, Klaus Heller.

View of the 1089ft Hörby Antenna in Sweden.
The tallest ladder I ever climbed. Photo, Anders Thulin.

Freefall in the vicinity of a 1089ft antenna. Photo, Jevto Dedijer.

Our magnificent Renault 4 ready for action. Photo, Jevto Dedijer.

Bernard, Scott and myself just before leaving for Germany and
Kochertalbrücke.

The terrifying Montparnasse Tower. Photo, A. Monier.

I check the view from the observation deck of the Montparnasse Tower.
Doesn't look fun. Photo, Scott Elder.

Packing my Strato Cloud on Avenue de Saxe in Paris.
Photo, Scott Elder.

30 minutes before I trip and fall head first from
the 693 ft Montparnasse Tower.
Photo, Jean-Pierre Lacroix.

The runway on top of the Montparnasse Tower. Photo, Jevto Dedijer.

Bernard hangs safely below his canopy while Scott steps off the edge.
Photo, Jean-Pierre Lacroix.

Scott in freefall over downtown Paris.
Photo, Jean-Pierre Lacroix.

Scott crashes head first into the windows on the 30th floor.
Photo, Jean-Pierre Lacroix.

Touchdown in Paris. Photo, Jean-Pierre Lacroix.

Bernard in New York.
Photo, Jevto Dedijer.

Scott posing in front of a T-38 in Del Rio, TX.
Photo, Jevto Dedijer.

Yolaine makes a tandem jump from 13,000ft attached to my friend
Anders Thulin (I just exited the aircraft). Photo, Per Svensson.

A Kamikaze Toast

I pushed Cloudia into the Fnac bag and placed a couple of T-shirts on top to hide her. Not that I thought the guards would inspect our luggage, but I would rather be safe than sorry. I had heard about the police in the United States confiscating BASE jumpers' parachutes if they caught them after landing. The parachute is a skydiver's most valuable possession and I was prepared to fight for mine. Bernard poured us each a drink, and we toasted each other and emptied the glasses. I thought about war movies I had seen: kamikaze pilots lifting their glasses in a last toast to the emperor before leaving on their deadly mission.

Inside my brain, a frantic battle was raging. One moment I felt happy and excited and the next I was fighting thoughts of death. I tried to banish the bad thoughts, but they kept popping up again and again.

It was 5:15 p.m. We were going to jump in 45 minutes. It was time to go. The Montparnasse Tower was a 20-minute walk from Avenue de Saxe. We did not talk much on the way. As we entered the hustle and bustle of Boulevard Montparnasse I had the feeling of being watched by the crowd. I felt like a prisoner on the run, as if they knew what we were up to and were about to arrest us. I pushed away these thoughts as complete nonsense. At once another discouraging thought came to mind: the similarity of our walk to the last walk from the holding cell on death row to the electric chair.

A group of teenagers was having fun roller-skating and skateboarding at the foot of the Tower. "Guys, stay for a while and you'll see something really cool," I wanted to say. The weather was perfect. It was a clear, cool evening with a light breeze of about 6.5 miles/hour, blowing in the right direction. The wind would be at our backs as we jumped which would help us stay as far away from the building as possible. Arin, Maria, and Helena were waiting by the entrance. I walked inside with Arin behind me. We took the elevator to the 56th floor and sat down in the bar. Bernard, Scott, Maria, and Helena would enter half an hour later and continue directly to the observation deck. This would be a signal to Arin and me. We would watch the elevator from our position in the bar and the moment we saw the others walk by, we would walk up to the roof. We didn't realize that we were actually complicating the jumps by behaving this way. Scott and I would come to regret it dearly. I jumped at the slightest movement from the guards and thought, "This is it. They'll take my parachute." Nothing happened. The elevator attendant recognized me and asked to which floor we were headed.

"The bar", I answered.

Arin carried my parachute and appeared calm and collected. After a rapid ascent, the elevator stopped on the 56th floor. The guards let us into the bar without as much as checking our tickets. We had cleared the first phase.

We sat down and ordered two Kronenbourg beers. I suddenly felt dizzy and began salivating and headed for the bathroom. Looking in the mirror, I was shocked. My face was white as a ghost. I rubbed my cheeks with ice-cold water in an attempt to recover my natural color. On my way back to the table, I was stopped by one of the guards. This time I was certain I would be arrested and prepared myself to wear handcuffs for the second time in my life. But as I looked at the guard I noticed he was smiling and wanted to ask me something.

"Monsieur, êtes vous joueur de basket-ball?" (Do you play basketball?) he asked politely. I have been asked this question several times a day since I was fifteen and normally become a little irritated. This time I appreciated the question and found it comical. I answered him that I did not play basketball, but was pretty good at chess. We could play some day if he was interested.

As the guard thought about this, I returned to the table and sat down by Arin. The others should certainly have been here by now. Where were they? My hands were perspiring heavily and I dried them frequently on my pants. Arin poked me on my leg and pointed to the elevator. There they were. I could hear the ticket inspectors commenting on Scott's backpack and mumbling something about stupid American tourists. They passed the guards and continued on to the deck; now it was time for Arin and me to follow. My heart was in overdrive and I thought it would explode, but at least I was no longer perspiring or nauseated.

Walking up the steps to the deck was very stressful. I climbed one step. Hesitated. Climbed another step. My legs weighed a ton. My body told me not to go, but my brain urged me on. What if I went to hide under a warm down comforter instead and read a good book. My soul was being torn apart. "What are you doing, Jevto?! Are you crazy? You can still change your mind." I arrived at a heavy metal door with the sign *"Terrasse d'observation"* in big red letters. The door was pulled open from the other side and before I could move I was nearly run over by a group of Japanese tourists. There were about 40 tourists on the deck. Once on deck, I could feel a sea of calm wash over me, the same feeling as before my jump from Kochertalbrücke. I felt at ease even though I still had the high fence to climb.

Bernard rolled out the rope and Arin extracted Cloudia from the Fnac bag. The tourists were still unaware of what was happening. Little kids were running around, laughing and playing while their parents admired the incredible view. I strapped on my parachute. Scott asked if I was ready. I gave him a nod. Bernard tied the rope around the fence, looked at Scott and me and began climbing. I could hear some of the tourists commenting, "What are they doing? Are they nuts? They can't climb that fence!"

I was standing with my back to the tourists and didn't feel like turning around. Only the jump was of importance now. Scott was climbing over. My turn would come soon. When Scott jumped from Montparnasse the first time, he noticed one of the sharp steel spikes on top of the fence was missing and that is where I put my foot when I vaulted over the fence. Vaulted might be too strong of a word. It was not easy getting over the high fence. The steel spikes were four inches long and if one of them had ended up in my abdomen I would have been cut open like a pig. I jumped down onto the metal roof, and stood firmly, at least for a little while. We left the rope for the girls to take care of.

We threw a roll of toilet paper from the roof to check the wind direction. It was still blowing in the same direction as on the ground. We were standing on a twenty-inch wide "runway" which would serve as our launch pad. The view was awesome. Far below us I could see cars and people, about the size of ants. Bernard was ready. He gave us one last glance and told us he would jump in 30 seconds. The roof "runway" was narrow and we had to watch our step.

I glanced over at the crowd and smiled. A few moments ago, these people had been admiring the view of Paris like normal tourists. Now they were our personal audience. Their eyes were wide with surprise. In the seriousness of it all, I did not realize that most of the spectators probably thought we were going to commit suicide.

Bernard backed up a little for a short running exit. I was standing behind him looking at his back and dark curly hair. The roof creaked when I walked on it. Everything seemed so unreal. Here I was with two of my good friends, 693 feet above ground, ready to leap off the edge of the building. Looking at my outfit, I had to laugh to myself. The poor spectators had to be confused. A businessman about to commit suicide together with an American tourist and a French student: not something you see every day. Bernard tightened his leg straps, grabbed the pilot chute with his right hand, and made a last equipment check. He gave us a quick glance, took four long steps, and jumped exuberantly into the air. He immediately disappeared from view.

Scott walked to the corner of the building, lay down on his stomach to see better, and reported that Bernard was hanging safely under his canopy. It was Scott's turn now. This time, he checked his equipment extra carefully to ensure everything was in order. He did not want to repeat the mistake which almost cost him his life in our night jump from Kochertalbrücke. He wanted to get as far away from the building as possible, so he picked a spot 30 feet from the corner. If he ran fast enough, he would reach a safe distance from the building. He wore a little white cap with the Eiffel Tower on it which he had purchased in a souvenir shop. Scott knew it would come off in the freefall, but kept it on as he felt it brought him luck. He gave me a thumbs-up, made a good exit, and disappeared into the void.

My turn was up. I waited for ten seconds to allow an adequate height difference between Scott and me. Mid-air crashes between jumpers have occurred simply because the second jumper did not wait long enough before jumping. I was surrounded by glass, metal, and steel; lampposts, traffic signs, and cars awaited me on the ground. It was not a serene environment. I noticed a pretty young lady around 25 with beautiful dark brown hair. Her warm smile gave me the extra encouragement I so badly needed.

"It's now or never!" I told myself. With the pilot chute in hand, I took off running across the narrow tin plate roof. Just before reaching the corner, I glanced down at my feet to avoid tripping on the roof. Unfortunately, this actually *caused* me to trip and fall off the Montparnasse Tower.

I left the roof deck of Montparnasse head-first. I was freefalling above Paris. What an incredible feeling. Between my legs I could see how the building rushed by me at high speed. After falling for two seconds, I looked down. I immediately got the incredible but frightening sensation of the ground coming toward me at a terrific speed. I counted to three and let go of my pilot chute. A second later, Cloudia unfolded with a bang, saving me once again. I looked down and saw Scott below me. The feeling of accomplishment was beyond description. Everything had worked out perfect...so far.

With a ram-air canopy, landings are supposed to be performed against the wind. Making a soft landing with a modern parachute is about as easy as getting out of bed in the morning. About 165 feet above ground, I realized I was going down-wind. For some reason I had forgotten to steer up against the wind. With my right hand on the toggle, I pulled hard and did a sharp turn. Just before hitting the ground I realized my landing would be more of a crash landing. The ground came rushing toward me with tremendous speed and the next thing I heard was the sound of my body hitting the ground. Boom! Smack! Crash!

When I opened my eyes I was on my back on the bottom of a stairwell, 16 feet below ground. The first thing I noticed was that I was still alive. I carefully moved my arms and legs and nothing seemed to be broken. Rainsy, my friend from Cambodia who had watched the jumps, came running. He had seen the landing and feared I might be dead. I gathered all the strength I had and stood up. I walked up the steps I had come barreling down earlier, pain shooting through my right leg. I was relieved to see Bernard, who told me with an urgent voice that Scott had hurt his foot and was not able to run. Now it was time to get away as quickly as possible.

Everything went so fast, I didn't have time to talk to Rainsy. Bernard and I ran toward the subway. Scott was not able to keep up and chose another escape route. We had agreed to meet in Scott's apartment in case something went wrong. Bernard and I didn't take the time to buy tickets; we just jumped the turnstiles. Finally sitting in one of the cars of the train, we hugged. The canopies were in our laps, but strangely enough none of the passengers noticed. It was difficult to get a good perspective of what had happened, it all went so fast.

I suddenly felt something warm trickling down my ankle. Slowly, I pulled up my right pant leg and gasped when I saw a big piece of muscle hanging outside of my calf. As calmly as possible, I told Bernard I had something to take care of and would make my way to Scott's apartment later. Of course he wondered why, and I pulled up my pant leg and pointed. Unfortunately, an older woman across from me saw my bloody leg and yelled, "Aaaaaaaahhhhhhh!"

She must have been one of those people who can not stand the sight of blood. Bernard told me about a good hospital near the Notre Dame cathedral. The cut in my leg looked nice and clean, as if someone had made an incision with a sharp knife. I thought about the brutal landing and remembered my right leg hit something hard just before I crash-landed on my back. We ran from the subway to try to find a taxi. It is not easy to find an empty cab during rush hour in Paris, but luck was on our side. I noticed a couple about to enter a cab. Showing my bloody leg I politely asked if they would consider letting us have the cab. At the sight of my injury, the husband pulled his wife out of the cab and a few minutes later I stumbled into the emergency department at Hôpital Hôtel-Dieu, leaning on Bernard.

I had lost quite a bit of blood and felt dizzy. The patient-count must have been low that evening, because five young staff members in white lab coats gathered around, questioning me. "How did this happen? Were you stabbed?"

My injury was discussed in medical terminology. I had been placed on an exam table for easier probing. My one sock was heavy with blood and considered ruined. It went directly into the garbage. I asked to speak to the doctor on call, but was told he could not be located. They examined the wound and tried to organize the mess before suturing. In answering the questions regarding what happened, I told them I had fallen in a subway escalator. It didn't seem to surprise them at all. I caught a glimpse of Bernard's face, which was alarmingly pale. Shortly thereafter, he left the room. He had seen too much blood.

When the white-clad staff began to discuss whether a tendon should go above or below a muscle, I became suspicious. My eyes caught an ID-badge, where I read the person's name and below it the word *Interne*. I looked at the others' ID-badges and they all said the same: *Interne*. What the hell! I was surrounded by students who didn't know what they were doing, and I was furious. Here I was with a serious injury and they didn't know where to place the tendon in relation to the muscle. I started yelling and swearing and demanded to see the doctor on call. He appeared in a few minutes. The doctor was around 40 years of age and dug in on my leg with confidence. For some reason he decided to suture the wound without anesthetic, which was not a very pleasant experience. The doctor noticed I was eager to be on my way and he worked fast. With 17 stitches in my leg, I limped to the waiting cab outside the hospital. During the short trip to Scott's apartment I thought about the mistake I had made and how easily I could have avoided ending up on my back in a stairwell.

The door to Scott's apartment was ajar and I could hear bluegrass music coming from inside. Bernard and I stepped in and found Scott sitting on his bed with one foot resting on a pillow. Maria, Arin, and Helena sat next to him, talking. When Scott saw us, he got up with great effort and hugged us both.

"We did it," he whispered in my ear.

Scott appeared to have a serious injury. His foot was swollen and blue in color. He was pale as a sheet and sweating. I sat down by him and showed off my injured leg. He laughed at my story about the students who didn't know where to place the tendon. Scott suspected his own foot was broken, but hoped that wasn't the case. He had previously broken the same foot twice, once when he was ten and fell down a stairway, and another time while downhill skiing. We thanked Maria, Helena, and Arin for their help and asked them to leave. We needed some time for male bonding.

Despite his injury, Scott took out his banjo and played a few tunes. We discussed our jumps from the Tower in more detail. Then Scott told us something that made my skin crawl. His exit had been successful, precisely according to Carl and Jean Boenish's recommendations, with head held high and eyes toward the horizon. After a four-second freefall, he had let go of his pilot chute. That is when it happened: the canopy opened directly toward the building and smashed him against a window. He pushed his feet against the building and managed to maneuver away from the window. After colliding with the building, Scott was not quite himself, and he made a careless landing. He could hear his foot crack the moment he landed. Craaak! Scott laughed at the thought of some secretary in the building who might have witnessed him flying toward her office window 330 feet above ground. How could she ever explain what she had seen? "Come quick! Someone is about to crash through my window!" Bernard, the least experienced of us, had made a perfect jump from exit to landing without even the slightest problem. All of us were physically and mentally exhausted after the adventure and looked forward to falling asleep in a warm, comfortable bed. Bernard went to his parents' home in Bailly, a Paris suburb. I stayed with Scott. We figured we might as well help each other out as we were both temporarily crippled. I told Scott my subway story, the made-up version I told the hospital staff. We agreed not to tell anyone else the truth about how we sustained our injuries. If we had to explain the entire story about our jumps to each and every one who asked, "What happened?" we would soon lose patience. We felt it was more practical to make up a story. After some discussion we came up with the following:

> "We were drinking rather heavily before we left for a party at the other end of the city. By the subway stairway, we began to wrestle for fun. We pushed each other and pulled each other's clothes. Approaching the stairway, Scott suddenly lost his balance. We both tumbled down the steep stairway. Scott broke his ankle and I cut my leg on the edge of a step."

That was what we would tell those who were curious enough to ask about our injuries. I worried that nobody would believe us, but we had to wait and see.

The following morning I awoke with terrible pain in my leg. It was stiff as a board and difficult to move. With Scott's help, I dragged myself to the bathroom. While I was brushing my teeth, I decided to tell Ylva Berthelson the true story. It would not be fair to lie to her. She had been kind enough to give me a day off to jump from Kochertalbrücke. All my fellow workers would hear the made-up version. I had to mobilize all my strength in order to get dressed. Never before had I experienced pain just from pulling on my socks.

I limped to the elevator, went down to the entry level, and stumbled out into the street. The subway was 1000 feet away and each step felt like it would be my last. I reached the subway as I was on the brink of fainting. After a bumpy ride in the morning rush hour I arrived at Facit.

The first person I encountered was Rainsy. He looked at me and asked if the injury was serious. I asked him to come with me to the bathroom and I would show him. Rainsy examined my wound while I rested my foot on the sink. He had extensive experience with all types of injuries from the Viet Nam war and estimated my time of recovery to four months. When Ylva heard my story, she reacted by laughing out loud. She could not believe I had jumped from the Montparnasse Tower. She said she had never heard anything so crazy in her whole life. When she eventually realized I was telling the truth, I was happy to hear her ask how it felt to freefall along the building and how many seconds I had fallen. Ylva did not know anything about BASE jumping, but was very interested in sports. She often went skiing and liked anything which was out of the ordinary.

Ylva let me know that somehow Facit's chief executive officer Stellan Horwitz had found out that I had jumped and injured myself. He wanted to see me in his office. Stellan Horwitz had been the CEO of the company for one year. He was tall and slender with dark brown hair. Mr. Horwitz was always dressed in elegant suits and wore French Weston shoes. I knocked on his office door and entered. He was behind his desk, hands folded on the polished desk top.

"Well," he began. "I have heard what you've been up to. You can't keep doing things like that. You have to understand I'm responsible for you while you work as a trainee here. You will simply have to act more responsibly."

I listened quietly to what he had to say. He realized I was in no shape to work and gave me two weeks leave of absence. As I walked out the door, he stopped me and asked, "Jevto, why did you do it? Why did you jump from that building?"

My eyes met his, and I answered that I did it to feel I was alive. I don't believe Stellan Horwitz ever understood why I jumped from the Montparnasse Tower and I had no desire to explain it further to him. That was the first and last time I spoke with CEO Stellan Horwitz.

When I returned to Avenue de Saxe that evening, I found Scott's apartment empty. His banjo was resting alone on the bed. The kitchen was a total mess. An empty box of painkillers which Scott and I had shared the previous night was on the floor. I presumed he had gone to the hospital for treatment of his foot. A few hours later he returned, looking like he had lost everything he owned and more. He sat down on the bed and sighed deeply. Hospital x-rays had shown that the bone structure of his foot looked more like a game of pick-up-sticks. When asked how many bones were broken, the doctors could only say, "A lot." Surgery was scheduled in a few days, when the foot would be reinforced with screws, pins, and bolts. Our little escapade would amount to a little more than 20,000 francs. The worst of it all was not the surgery itself, but that he had been told by a well-known sports physician that he would not be able to run again, much less sky-dive.

Scott did not have enough money for the surgery and hesitated for a long time before he decided to ask Yves Saint-Laurent for help. He was relieved to find that Yves would lend him the money to be paid back later. The surgery had to be performed as soon as possible as two days had already passed since the accident. Scott was admitted to Hôpital Américain, a hospital where some physicians specialized in sports injuries. They meticulously examined his foot to figure out how to put it together again.

As Scott prepared for surgery, I went to Hôtel-Dieu twice a week for dressing changes of my wound. The nurses were friendly and competent. After only a few days without moving my injured leg, I could feel how I slowly but surely lost control of my leg muscles to atrophy. I borrowed crutches from the hospital and with their help I was able to maneuver anywhere I wanted to.

The first time I visited Scott at the hospital, I was surprised at the Spartan furnishings. I had always equated private hospitals with luxury institutions, but this was not the case here. Scott's room was small with whitewashed walls. Besides the bed, there were two wooden chairs for visitors and a small nightstand. Scott brightened like the sun when he saw me. His leg was in a cast up to his knee and elevated in the air. Scott was pale but in good spirits. The food was so bad he had refused to eat for two days, the nurses were mean, and the patient in the room next door hated him. When he thought of the 20,000 francs price tag for this misery, he had to laugh at the situation. The neighbor disliked him because he had started playing his banjo on the first day. He supposedly threatened to kill Scott if he didn't stop playing his "American Western music."

I had brought a bag full of goodies for Scott: a six-pack of Pilsner Urquell, grapes, oranges, dried apricots, and the International Herald Tribune. Scott spent his time in the hospital writing down his thoughts and feelings in his green journal. We talked about what it is that makes certain people gladly jump from buildings. Neither one of us had a good answer.

Many people I have talked to feel it is an expression of suicidal tendencies, wishing for a quick end to life. I believe it is the total opposite. Making a BASE jump is a way to feel that one is really alive. One second you're standing up there, nervous, afraid, concentrating, and a short while later you have the firm ground beneath your feet. It is like leaving the earthly life for a short time to return a moment later in one piece (hopefully!). I think it is the awareness of one's mortality that makes skydiving, and BASE jumping in particular, such an exciting sport. High-risk sports such as skydiving, SCUBA diving, and mountain climbing are practiced by a minority group of adventure-seeking individuals. Of Sweden's population of 8.5 million, only 3000 practice skydiving. I don't think this number will ever increase much, just because skydiving is a sport for people with a certain outlook on life. It is interesting to note that those who practice a high-risk sport are very much alike, mentally. Research has shown that skydivers, mountain climbers, divers, fighter pilots, etc. share a joy of living and are uncomplicated and enterprising. On the negative side, it is said they like to drink copious amounts of alcohol and experiment with various drugs. Scott and I were not interested in answering the question of why skydiving and BASE jumping excited us, but rather what it was that makes certain people interested in high-risk sports. Perhaps we had it programmed in our DNA?

I visited Scott in the hospital every other day. One day I noticed a huge bouquet of flowers on his night stand. Next to the flowers were three big, beautiful books about Cezanne, Manet, and Turner. Scott explained that Yves Saint-Laurent and his business partner, Pierre Bergé, had paid an unexpected visit. They had also brought him a box of dark Belgian chocolates. Scott told me how Pierre Bergé had asked again and again if he had really injured himself by jumping from the Montparnasse Tower. When he finally grasped the truth, he stated with a laugh that he had never heard anything so out of this world in his entire life.

After two weeks in the hospital Scott's mood had improved, not because the hospital had become more hospitable, but because the discharge date was approaching. One evening as we discussed our jumps from Montparnasse, Scott looked straight into my eyes and said, "Jevto, you know what? We certainly messed up." (Understatement of the year) "We never once talked about the landing when we planned the jumps. That's why we screwed up."

We had made an unforgivable mistake. We had made the same mistake twice. The mistake was that we acted paranoid. We had spent more time trying to avoid being arrested than we had in planning the jump itself. The problem was in our heads, not in real life.

It is okay to make mistakes, but not the same one twice. If I were to make any more BASE jumps, my personal safety would have to come first and the risk of being arrested second. When jumping from an airplane one can enjoy more than two minutes below the canopy before landing. Plenty of time to plan and choose a landing site. The jump from the Montparnasse Tower lasted only 25 seconds: four seconds of freefall and 20 seconds below the canopy. It is important to start preparing for landing as soon as the canopy deploys. There is not even one second to spare. The landing site has to be carefully and precisely chosen beforehand.

Both Scott and I had made serious misjudgments. I had planned my landing a few seconds before I crashed into the stairwell. On top of this, I had made a sharp turn too close to the ground, the worst thing you can do with a ram-air canopy. It was a wonder I didn't break all the bones in my body. Scott's foot injury was not exactly the result of misjudgment, but of his brutal landing when he twisted his foot. Even more serious was the fact that he had crashed into the building. The suspension lines had become twisted as the canopy opened and blocked the steering lines. Heading straight for the building with blocked steering lines, there was not much he could do to avoid the crash. Scott was lucky his canopy didn't collapse against the building. Had he been careless during the packing of his chute? Only Scott could answer that question and I doubted that he even knew the answer.

Scott's doctor had confirmed that his repaired foot had to be protected from stress and said it could easily break again if he was careless. Scott decided to land on one leg, his left, in future skydives. There was no question that he would continue his favorite sport.

After two weeks of rest, I returned to Facit. My leg was improving but I was still unable to bear weight on my foot. Rainsy assisted with physical therapy during lunch breaks. I sat on a chair while Rainsy held my foot with strong hands. As he offered resistance, I tried to push my leg toward the floor. Then we did the same exercise in the opposite direction. I tried to lift my leg while Rainsy's hands resisted. These were simple but very effective exercises. After more than two weeks rest, my leg looked like a half-rotten vanilla pod. The muscles had been resting for a long time and longed for some training.

Rumors about my escapades had spread to all the departments at Facit. Whether I went downstairs to the warehouse or upstairs to marketing, the same thing happened. Everybody knew. I could hear how they whispered behind my back, "Look. There's that crazy trainee. I hear he jumped from a building."

I continued to visit the nurses at Hôtel-Dieu one afternoon a week for a change of dressing for my wound. During one of the visits I chatted with a physician who informed me that I had been very lucky. He explained I had been three-eighths of an inch from losing the use of my leg below the knee. The injury was very close to the main tendon between the thigh and calf muscle.

The treatment at the hospital was free, but I still called my parents in Lund to ask for help with money. I had lost two weeks' pay because of my leave from work and was unable to earn any extra cash. My parents did not know about my jump from Kochertalbrücke and I had no intention of telling them about the jumps from the Montparnasse Tower. Not yet. I called them one evening after work. My mother answered.

"Hi Mom, it's Jevto. How are you doing?"

"We're fine, and you?" she asked.

"Well, I've hurt my leg a little. It's nothing serious, but I'm wondering if…"

My mother cut in before I could finish the sentence. "What happened, Jevto?" she asked in a worried voice. "Tell me, Jevto."

I had decided on the subway version and tried to tell it with as much feeling as possible. "Well, Scott and I fell in a stairway in the subway and hurt ourselves. I have some sutures in my leg, but like I said, it's not serious."

She was quiet. Didn't she believe me? "You know what? I'll fly to Paris tomorrow to take care of you. You need someone to cook for you and to clean."

I thought. I didn't want my mother to go through all this trouble just because I had a few stitches in my leg. If she came to Paris I would not be able to hide the truth. I would have to tell her we had jumped from the Montparnasse Tower. "No thanks, Mom, that's not at all necessary! I get along just fine. But I would appreciate if you could help me with some money," I continued.

"Of course we will, my darling. But are you sure you don't want me to come to Paris? I would be happy to help you."

"Yes, I'm absolutely sure. Scott and I take care of each other."

"You know what?' she said. "I'll send you some money tomorrow. How much do you need?"

"Fifteen hundred francs would be enough," I answered.

"Okay, Jevto. I'll tell Dad to go to the bank tomorrow and send you a check. Get well soon and promise to call if you need anything." I promised her I would.

I hung up and sat down on my bed. I had done it. I had actually lied to her. My relationship with my parents had always been very open and honest and it didn't feel right to lie to them, but in this case I felt I had to. I wanted to make more BASE jumps and didn't want to worry them unnecessarily. When the time was right, I would tell them about our adventure from beginning to end.

The Hunt is on

My injured leg had finally recuperated enough to bear my weight, so I was able to walk without crutches again, albeit slowly. Scott's cast was to come off soon. We were ready to begin planning our next BASE jump. Why did we insist on putting ourselves in danger again after being injured the last time? Our shared sense of adventure drove us to it. We were stuck in a web of adrenaline. Once again the Eiffel Tower came up in discussions about possible objects. Would we be able to maintain enough distance from the tower during freefall?

The Eiffel Tower is a magical tower. It is the first thing that comes to mind when a foreigner thinks about Paris. I don't think any other building in the world is so loved by so many people. Think what you want, but Paris would not be Paris without its Eiffel Tower. Not a single person died during the construction of the tower, which is astounding when you consider the relatively primitive technology of the late 1800s. However, people have been coming here to die since the very first day the tower opened to the public. As of this writing, over 430 people have committed suicide by jumping from the deck 915 feet above ground. In 1963, a Spanish man threw his wife off the third floor after a violent argument. The woman, who was fairly heavy, is said to have made a considerable impression in the ground below.

We knew there was a fence on top of the tower, installed to keep people from jumping, but we didn't think it would be impossible to climb if we really wanted to. We rode up the Eiffel Tower elevator together to explore the possibility of a successful jump. (This was before the American B.J. Worth jumped from the tower as a stand-in for Grace Jones in the James Bond movie "A View to a Kill.") The view was incredible. There were plenty of opportunities for a good landing in the Champs de Mars Park and its sprawling lawn below. We realized that the jump would technically be only slightly more difficult than our jumps from the Montparnasse Tower. Scott was excited and in favor of the Eiffel Tower. I hesitated. I wanted to make my next BASE jump in peaceful and quiet surroundings. I suppose I was jittery after my crash landing.

After debating for a few days, I notified Scott and Bernard that I did not want to jump from the Eiffel Tower. They accepted my decision and the hunt for another object began. We had agreed to find an object that all three of us would accept.

Bernard came up with the excellent idea of looking for suitable objects in the big library at the Georges Pompidou cultural center. The cultural center caused quite a controversy when it was built. It is an extremely modern building rising from the midst of the old market halls of Paris, prominently featuring a glass-enclosed escalator on its exterior that brings visitors up and into the building.

We began looking under the reference "modern architecture." We noted with great interest that there were about 30 antennas of 1000 feet or more in France alone. Bernard informed us that they were all very well guarded. Each antenna is surrounded by a high fence. The antenna guard and his family live in a house within the fence. One or two German Shepherds, trained to attack, are standard. I was not interested in having to use bolt cutters and wrestling German Shepherds.

Scott found something else interesting, a dam in Switzerland. It was a concrete dam located in a small village called Mauvoisin, 660 feet high and seemingly ideal for a jump. The next page in the book showed a photo of a 760-foot dam in Dixence, also in Switzerland. We discussed the classification of a dam. Building or bridge? According to Scott, building was the only possibility. We decided that Scott would contact a man by the name of Tim Bruchauser in Bern. He had made 65 BASE jumps and was familiar with Switzerland. Perhaps he had jumped from one of the dams?

We continued our search as we didn't want to limit ourselves to dams. In addition to Trollveggen in Norway, there was El Capitan, the cliff in Yosemite National Park from which Carl Boenish had made his initial BASE jumps. It is 3000 feet high and slightly overhung; ideal for BASE jumps. The problem was that it was far away and we did not have money for the trip. Scott and Bernard sat on the floor between two rows of books, each searching for a suitable object. Scott broke the silence. "I found something cool. A 1000-feet-high cliff in England."

I went over to look at the photo and quickly realized that he was joking. The cliff slanted outward. If we didn't crash into it after 30 feet of freefall, we would certainly be crushed after 60 feet. The cliff slanted straight down into the sea. I could see myself being pulled under the water with the canopy over my body, heavy from the water.

I tired of looking in books and sat down in a comfortable easy chair. Closing my eyes, I let my thoughts wander freely. I thought about Skåne and its beautiful landscape. When I was 12, my parents owned a summer home in the middle of the dense forest. One of my favorite pastimes was building huts in the forest. I sawed, cut, braided, and dug until I had constructed a little cubbyhole that would have withstood any storm, or so I thought. When I wasn't building huts, I fished in a small creek running close to the house. I could sit for hours and watch the homemade fly bob on the surface. Every once in a while it would be pulled down below the surface by a little brook trout. I was quick to set the hook and I often brought home a couple of trout after a day of fishing. The forest had a rich animal life with both big and small creatures. There were plenty of deer, sometimes wandering all the way up to our window out of curiosity. Nature and its secrets were just outside our door.

Without realizing it, my thoughts about the natural beauty of Skåne blended together with the reason I was sitting in an easy-chair in the library: BASE jumping. Would it be possible to make a BASE jump in Sweden? I made a mental list of all possible objects I could think of in Sweden. The bridge between Kalmar and Öland was in a beautiful location, but probably not quite high enough. It would turn out to be more of a dive than a BASE jump. There were no suitable mountains in Sweden. What about antennas? Most of them are protected by dense impenetrable forest, which would make landing impossible. No, we needed an antenna in an open field, not too close to populated areas.

The Hörby antenna! Why hadn't I thought of it before? The antenna was perfect, just what we were looking for. It was located about 20 miles northeast of Lund, in the middle of Skåne's flatland. I wasn't exactly sure how high it was but I presumed it reached close to 1000 feet above ground, high enough for a BASE jump. I shared my idea with Bernard and Scott and both found it interesting. We left the library and entered a small bar in the same block to continue our discussion. Naturally, we wanted to gather as much information as possible about the antenna before we jumped. How high was it? How many cables were used to hold it in place? Was it guarded? Would we be able to hot-wire the elevator so we didn't have to climb the ladder all the way up? We had a lot of questions and we wanted answers, fast.

I called a friend in Malmö, Herbert Södergren, who I thought might be able to help with the answers regarding the Hörby antenna. Herbert and I first met at the Skåne Skydiving Club. He was an instructor with almost 700 jumps, but no BASE jumps. I called him one evening and explained our plans to jump from the Hörby antenna. Herbert was surprised to say the least, but promised to help by investigating the antenna. I also asked him to take a few photos of the antenna to show Scott and Bernard. Two weeks later a thick envelope arrived from Herbert containing the information we had requested.

With the help of aviation maps, Herbert had figured out the antenna's height to be 1,089 feet. However, it was uncertain if we would be able to climb that high as the last 100 to 130 feet of an antenna structure usually consist of the TV antenna itself. An eight-foot high fence surrounded the antenna, but did not appear too difficult to climb. Three sets of cable secured the antenna. This was very important; it meant that we had 120 degrees between each cable, leaving us plenty of room. A smaller grove of trees near the antenna could serve as a hiding place for our car while we jumped. Herbert had also found out that the employees usually left the location about 5 p.m. Weekends, the place was empty of people. The only thing he had not been able to find out was whether the elevator could be hot-wired. Herbert had noticed it at the bottom of the antenna, but did not want to risk getting caught messing with the elevator buttons. We put the elevator problem off for later.

Each time we planned a BASE jump, we allowed our black humor to flow freely. We met, drank a few beers and joked about death. "Can I have your stereo if you get killed?" or "Do you want me to ship your body to your mother if you are crushed to death?" It may seem callous to joke about death, but for us it was a way to get used to the fact that our sport was dangerous and bad things could happen. It was important for us to keep a certain distance from what we were doing.

I realized that the risk of injuring myself badly a second time was relatively high. We were the pioneers of a sport which was barely taking its first stumbling steps in Europe, and pioneers have to be prepared to take great risks.

For a long time we had tried to think of a name for our team. What should we call ourselves? Suggestions such as "the BASE-gang," "the BASE-boys," and "the BASE trio" had been decided against because they were too boring. We needed an exciting name with some spirit and oomph. Someone suggested "The Idiots' Club" and we all thought it was a perfect name. Easy to pronounce, short, descriptive, and stupid enough that people would wonder what it was all about. We decided to use the name in the press if and when any journalist was ever interested in doing a story about us.

Before we left for Sweden and the Hörby antenna, we decided to take a week's vacation, separately. My mother had told me that my younger brother Miki and my father were vacationing in the small fishing village of Trsteno, located 18 miles north of the medieval city of Dubrovnik, on the Adriatic Coast of Croatia. We had gone there every summer since I was five.

My father was born 1911 in Sarajevo. After finishing school in Yugoslavia and Italy, he went to the United States to study theoretical physics at Princeton. One of the more memorable events in the United States was when he threw a snowball at Einstein, whose office was next door to Dad's classroom. Dad never mentioned whether Einstein threw a snowball back at him or not. After some time as a paratrooper in the 101st Airborne, he returned to Yugoslavia where he married Ivanka. They had two children, Lada and Danica. His marriage to Ivanka lasted ten years. Then he made a trip to the United States, married a woman there by the name of Polly, divorced her a year later and returned to Europe. For more than 30 years, I have tried to obtain more information about Polly from my father, but her name is still the only thing I know.

In the late 1950s, Tito decided that Yugoslavia would produce an atomic bomb. My father was selected as project leader, but immediately came into conflict with Tito. When Tito noticed that dad was deliberately delaying the project, he took revenge by imposing travel restrictions and subjecting Dad to other harassment such as anonymous phone calls in the middle of the night and frequent visits by the police. Dad turned to a physicist friend in Sweden for help. The physicist Torsten Gustavsson, an adviser to Swedish Prime Minister Tage Erlander, came to the rescue, and with the skilful application of some political pressure managed to bring dad to Scandinavia in 1960. He obtained a job at the Niels Bohr Institute in Copenhagen, which is where he met wife number three, Carin Birgitta Hallberg. They were married in 1961. Two years later their first son, me, was born, and after another two years their second son, Miki, saw the light of day. We traveled to Yugoslavia as often as we could so Miki and I would not lose contact with our father's homeland and our half-sisters Lada and Danica.

The journey to Croatia was long. After a 36-hour trip by train and bus I finally stood in front of Trsteno's pride, an enormous plane tree, and was overwhelmed with joy. I had not been in Croatia for three years. I followed a winding path to the ocean. It was a wonderful day. The sun shone from a clear blue sky and the air smelled of sea and cypress.

The wonderful fragrances mostly stemmed from the Arboretum, a beautiful park which surrounded the village. At the end of the 1700s, a botanist began importing plants and trees from various places in the world and now, more than 200 years later, hundreds of different varieties can be found in this park. I headed for a small café in the marina and spotted Miki and Dad sitting in the shadow, each with a glass of white wine. I surprised them by sitting down at a table next to them and asking if we could have lunch together, as if it were the most natural thing in the world. Neither Dad nor Miki had seen me enter the café and were so surprised they were at a loss for words. We hugged each other and excitedly began sharing our stories and experiences from the past year.

Miki had been living in the United States for the past few years. He was studying at Princeton to become a physician. When we last saw each other he was just under six feet tall and very slim. Now he looked like a first-class athlete. He had grown about an inch in height, but had made great gains in muscle mass. Miki told us he was a member of the school's rowing team and practiced twice a day. As if his Schwarzenegger-like muscles were not enough, his trainer had asked him to gain another 17 pounds in pure muscle weight. Miki is very romantically inclined and has no problem picking up the most beautiful women. He looks at them with poetically yearning eyes from behind his round John Lennon eyeglasses and that's all it takes. Once they're hooked, they won't leave him alone for a moment. He was eager for the opportunity to socialize with European women more intimately during his stay.

After lunch, we all stretched out in the sunshine and I began the process of frying my spooky white skin. It felt wonderful to lay on my back in the warm sun and not have to think about anything at all. Every once in a while we cooled off with a swim in the crystal clear water.

Toward the end of my week in Trsteno, I received a letter from my mother. Even before opening it I suspected it was very important, since she had written to me in Croatia. I was shocked when I opened the envelope and saw the contents. My mother had cut out a few newspaper articles from various Swedish daily papers. One headline read: "Carl Boenish, well-known skydiver, falls to his death in Norwegian mountains!" I glanced through the article. *Kvällsposten* wrote, "Carl Boenish fell to his death yesterday morning when he attempted a jump from Stabben in the Trollveggen mountains..." I sat on the edge of the bed with the article in my hand. How could this have happened? How could the Father of BASE jumping get killed? I knew I could not get the answers from the newspaper articles. Reading the articles, I got the impression that the journalists had neither the interest nor the time to research the subject fully. What surprised me the most was my mother's letter. She wrote:

"My little darling.

How are you doing in Paris? I'm sending you a few clippings about an accident which happened a few days ago in Norway. I hope you don't jump from Trollveggen! It's too dangerous!

Love, Mom."

Did my mother suspect something? Did she know I had already made BASE jumps and planned to make more? I realized I would soon have to tell her what I was doing; there was no point in keeping it a secret any more.

Shortly after my return from Croatia I had a surprise visit from my father. He called me from the Charles de Gaulle airport just north of Paris, and asked if we could have lunch. He was on a two-day business trip and wanted to see me. We agreed to meet at the home of one of his very good friends, Cy Sultzberger, on Boulevard Montparnasse. On my way there, I realized this was the opportunity I had been waiting for. Cy Sultzberger lives only a stones-throw from the Montparnasse Tower and the entire building is visible from his kitchen window, as I recalled from a previous visit. Dad and Cy were sitting in the living room drinking Irish whisky I arrived. The first thing I did was sign my name in the guest book. Cy is very particular about this. He insists that everybody who pays him a visit sign the book.

Cy, whose family owns the New York Times, was a foreign correspondent for the newspaper for many years. He has met the statesmen of the world; Tito, Eisenhower, Mao Zedong, Carter, Ford, Ghandi, Brezhnev, de Gaulle, and Khadaffi to name just a few. The walls of one of the hallways in his apartment were covered with photos, all personally signed with words like, "To my friend Cy from…"

The lunches at Cy's are always fantastic, thanks to his Bosnian housekeeper. After the delicious lunch and coffee with a big glass of cognac, I was about to fall asleep on the couch, but both Dad and I had to leave. We thanked Cy for the lunch and left. I suggested a walk along Boulevard Montparnasse to settle our stomachs. About level with the Montparnasse Tower, I nonchalantly told Dad I had jumped from the building. Dad's mind was on other things and he didn't hear me. I repeated myself, a little louder this time. He looked at me and smiled, as if I had told a funny story. I asked him to stop walking, turned his head toward the Montparnasse Tower and said loudly and clearly, "Dad! Scott, Bernard, and I have jumped from the Montparnasse Tower."

He looked at me in surprise and said, "Really?! You really did that?"

I convinced him I was telling the truth and then he surprised me. He took my hand and congratulated me on my jump. He said he was very proud of me, but couldn't understand how I had brought myself to do it. "I would never dare make such a jump," he confessed.

I explained to dad that the members of the Idiots' Club had plans to jump from the Hörby antenna and possibly Trollveggen. He listened to me without interrupting or commenting. We decided it would be best if I told Mom myself.

I felt an enormous relief after I told my father about my BASE jumps, like a ship that had just weighed anchor.

Jacob's Ladder

Bernard, Scott, and I met at the Idiots' Club clubhouse on Avenue de Saxe for our first meeting since our short vacation. After a very long discussion, Bernard and I made the decision to jump from Trollveggen. We were aware of the danger, that Carl Boenish had been killed, but we both thought it was worth a try. We each bought an Interrail card and Scott purchased a one-way ticket from Paris to Copenhagen and another from Copenhagen to New York. Scott had already made three jumps from Trollveggen and didn't feel like cheating death once again. Bernard and I would continue to Trollveggen after completing our jumps from the Hörby antenna.

We packed our backpacks in Scott's apartment: underwear, a stack of T-shirts, toiletries, mosquito repellent, and parachutes. Just as we were about to leave in a cab for the railroad station, Scott decided to write a letter to his grandmother in the United States. He finished the letter and we had to jump the train as it was gaining speed. I don't think I have ever been on time for anything in Scott's company. He is a true master of procrastination.

The train ride to Sweden was wonderful, at least for Scott and Bernard. The train was full of tanned, blonde Swedish women on their way home from vacation. I have always preferred dark French and Italian women, so I stayed out of the competition. The trip was unusually uneventful considering the three of us were together. We fell asleep about midnight and didn't wake up until the train stopped at the Copenhagen *Hovedbangård* (Central Station) in the morning. Bernard was especially excited, as this was his first time in Scandinavia. We took the hydrofoil to Malmö where Herbert was waiting for us. He drove straight downtown to Skydive Skåne's clubhouse, where he had made sure there were sheets on the beds and food and beer in the refrigerator. We shaved and showered to wash off the travel-dust.

We had a bit to eat and then sat down to discuss the next day's jump. Herbert had explained in his letter that he was interested in jumping from the Hörby antenna himself and we welcomed his initiative. As we began to plan, we were surprised to find that Herbert had a different opinion on how to pull off the jump. He insisted on climbing the antenna at night and jumping at dawn. Listening to Herbert's suggestion, red flags immediately popped up in my brain. "Watch out, Jevto. Don't complicate another BASE jump. Remember KISS." Scott reacted with an outburst of anger over Herbert's idea.

"We're not going to spend a whole goddamn night on top of a TV-antenna just because you're afraid to get caught by the Swedish police!" he yelled.

I tried to calm them down. This was not a good time for internal conflicts. Arguing would only lead to distraction and carelessness and with those ingredients anything could happen. To a certain extent, I could understand Herbert's feelings. This would be his first BASE jump and he was obviously nervous. Besides, he was afraid he would lose his skydiving license if he was arrested. On the other hand, I felt that as we had the most experience in BASE jumping, Herbert should leave the organizing to us. I suggested we take a look at the antenna before we jumped.

We drove the 19 miles to Hörby at high speed. Conversation in the car ceased as we neared the antenna. The sun was shining from a clear blue sky over the Skåne countryside. A narrow, winding road carried us through the forest for some time until we arrived at an opening and there, straight ahead of us, towered the Hörby antenna, more than 1,050 feet tall. I stepped out of the car and stared at it. It seemed so low. Perhaps Herbert was mistaken about the height? The fence he had told us about stretched all the way around the antenna, 165 feet from the base. Unlike the fence on the top the Montparnasse Tower, here there were no sharp spikes to worry about. We would have plenty of landing sites to choose from; green, flat fields surrounded the antenna except on one side, where the forest was dense. The elevator was parked at the bottom and I doubted we would be able to hot-wire it. We simply lacked the technical skill. The only possibility was that someone had forgotten their keys inside the elevator, which was a long-shot. If we couldn't ride the elevator, we would have to climb the ladder all the way. It was without a doubt the tallest ladder I would ever set foot on. Still, we didn't know how high we would be able to climb. We might have to jump from 660 feet if the passage was blocked for some reason. We had seen what we wanted to see. The antenna was still standing and there were plenty of places to land. We had not heard a word from Herbert the entire time. He seemed deep in his own thoughts, probably wondering what he had gotten himself into.

Back in Malmö, we packed our canopies on the lawn. I know Cloudia was anxious to fly as she had been confined inside the container since the flight from the Montparnasse Tower. I had washed her to get rid of the bloodstains from my leg injury. I packed, pulled, and stowed. I had the BASE packing technique down pat now and usually finished in less than 30 minutes. When I had finished my own packing I helped Herbert with advice regarding his packing.

Herbert had made a phone call to a friend who agreed to drive the car to and from the antenna. His name was Micke and he had 30 skydives under his belt. One thing was sure: he had never witnessed a jump from a TV antenna before. Micke was studying mechanical engineering at the University of Lund while working at a glue-factory on weekends. The reasons we didn't want to drive the car ourselves were both practical and self-serving. Practical, because escape would be quicker with a driver than if one of us had to take off the rig and get behind the wheel. Self-serving, because when the adrenaline is running through the blood, all you want to do is scream for joy, drink champagne, hug your friends, and have a good time. Sitting behind the steering wheel is not on the list.

In the evening, Herbert took us to The Good Old Days Restaurant in Malmö. The restaurant is decorated like a British pub and has a French specialty on the menu: deep-fried Camembert with cloudberry jam. I have no idea where this dish originated, but I insisted it was French. Bernard suspected that the waiter was joking when he carried in a piece of fried Camembert, sprinkled some parsley over it and topped it with a spoonful of cloudberry jam. Bewildered, he looked at me and I nodded, letting him know he should give it a try. Bernard shook his head, tried a microscopic piece of cheese and handed me his plate. He explained that for a minute he suspected he was being filmed for a Candid Camera-type show, and that the entire Swedish population would be laughing at the stupid Frenchmen.

We each ordered a beer before the lottery ceremony. I suggested Bernard should be responsible for the drawing. This time, I was surprised to find I was in luck. I drew the number one ticket. Herbert was to jump after me, followed by Bernard and then Scott. We stayed at the restaurant long enough to finish a few more beers.

Back at the clubhouse we went straight to bed, but none of us slept well that night. I dreamed I was being crushed against the thick steel cables which hold the antenna erect. One dream featured my mother, busily picking mushrooms in the woods when she suddenly came upon my partly decomposed body, still attached to the parachute. No. It would be too tragic to die at the age of 21. This was not my turn to go.

The alarm went off at 5:30 a.m. The atmosphere was somewhat subdued, mostly because Scott and Bernard hated getting out of bed that early. We had a light breakfast, consisting of a bun with butter and cheese and a glass of juice. Meanwhile, Micke got the car ready for us to load our parachutes. Blackbirds were singing, and judging from the sky, it would be a warm summer day. Driving down the highway toward Hörby, we played one of our favorite songs, Frankie Goes to Hollywood's "Relax, don't do it." I get nervous every time I hear it. "What if the singer Holly Jonsson is right? Maybe I shouldn't jump from the antenna today?"

I had begun penetrating the strange world I personally call the borderland. The feeling of existing in a land where life and death flow together, a land where the line between life and death is practically non-existent. You are about to do something which could be the last thing you do, but at the same time you are still participating in daily life with cheese sandwiches, gas stations, and newspapers. The feeling is very difficult to explain in words. Try a jump from a TV antenna and you will understand what I mean.

Bernard, Scott, and I yelled and hollered in the back seat in an effort to reduce the tension building inside us. I think Herbert felt somewhat like an outsider, considering our strong friendship. Micke drove the car, deep in thought and very quiet. He had barely said a word since we got out of bed. I would have given my left leg to know what was going on in his head. It must feel strange to be in the company of people who would rather jump from a TV antenna on a peaceful Sunday morning than stay in bed with a good book.

Micke broke his silence and informed us it was quite windy. I looked out the window and noticed a flag at a gas station standing straight out like a spear. I sincerely hoped the wind would not develop into a storm. We arrived at the antenna shortly after seven. Micke parked the car in the woods close to the antenna. We strapped on our chutes, checked the wind direction relative to the antenna and picked alternative landing sites. The idea is to know where to land if for some reason the predetermined landing site is inaccessible. The wind was fairly strong, but not too strong. I was very hesitant about jumping in wind speeds of more than 20 mph., when the risk for hard landings and injuries is significant.

We asked Micke to stay by the car. His job was to watch the car and, in the event someone was hurt, drive to the hospital as quickly as possible. I was the first man over the fence, closely followed by Bernard, Scott, and Herbert. We were barely on the other side of the fence before an incident happened. Bernard's pilot chute came out of its pocket and fell to the ground, where I unknowingly stepped on it. Unaware of what had happened, Bernard continued forward, thereby pulling his carefully packed canopy from its container. All four of us stopped in our tracks and stared at the chute on the ground. Darn! This was not good. Bernard remained calm. He kneeled by the canopy and shoved it back into the container. There was no doubt in my mind that his hasty packing could lead to serious injury. "His canopy will open in a mess, if it opens at all," I thought. "He'd better not get hurt." None of us said a word. Our personal safety was up to each one of us.

Bernard had finished repacking and we headed for the elevator. We inspected the buttons and pushed every single one without result. Unfortunately, we would have to climb all the way up the narrow ladder. It was a tall, metal ladder leading straight up to the sky. The metal was ice-cold. The horizontal metal steps were placed 16 inches apart. Our flexibility was very limited due to the parachutes on our backs. I jumped up and reached the first step. The metal felt terribly cold and we had forgotten to bring gloves. I took the lead and began climbing, pulling myself up step by step. Frequently, my parachute got caught in the railing behind me, so I leaned in as much as possible to avoid getting stuck.

At 165 feet, the view of Skåne's flat land was already magnificent. We covered the first few hundred feet quickly and without much effort, keeping track of our progress with the help of the cables. The cables were 165 feet apart; all we had to do was multiply the number of cables by 165 and we arrived at the height in feet. By the time we reached 330 feet, my hands were numb from the cold. Bernard complained he was cold, too, and asked me to speed up. By the third cable or 495 feet, I had to stop again to admire the view. I wondered if perhaps some farmer below had noticed us, and if so, what he was thinking.

"They sure are hard workers, those antenna-people. It's 7 o'clock on a Sunday morning, and they're already at work!"

By this time, I had grown tired. We had been climbing for 25 minutes and I felt the strain in my arm muscles. Another irritating factor was the thirst; my mouth was dry as sandpaper. I stopped again just below the 825-foot mark and told Herbert that we were now at the same height as Kochertalbrücke in Germany. He looked at me and shook his head in disbelief. "How could you even think of jumping from such a low height? You don't even have time to use the reserve chute," he hollered.

I laughed out loud, and I laughed until my stomach hurt. Here we were, looking at each other, 825 feet above ground on our way up a 1,089-foot-high TV antenna. It was Sunday, early morning, and I was kindly being referred to as a crazy man. But everything is relative, as the saying goes. Crazy depends on who you are compared with. A person who does not skydive would probably consider it just as crazy to jump from 1,089 feet as from 825 feet. Herbert could not understand why I was laughing and became irritated. I continued to climb, tears of laughter running down my cheeks.

I suddenly noticed something alarming about 30 feet above my head: a heavy-looking metal cover. I couldn't believe my eyes. Was this as high as we would get? I notified Herbert, Scott, and Bernard of my discovery. We agreed our only chance to continue was to move to the outside of the antenna. Jumping would have been adventure enough; now an angry God wanted us to climb on the outside, too. I didn't like it, but with clenched teeth, I swung my legs around the antenna and placed myself on the outside. I was sweating profusely. My pulse increased and my heartbeat felt like bouncing bowling balls in my chest. Luckily, we only had to climb a short distance on the outside and very soon we were all inside the antenna structure again.

We reached the 900-foot mark. The wind had increased in strength. Threatening black clouds rolled in from the south. "Just as long as it doesn't start to rain," I thought. I was sick of climbing. My body ached, especially around my shoulders and arms. This was the first time I actually longed to make a BASE jump. I wanted to get off the damn antenna and looked forward to the freefall.

It suddenly felt as if we were in the middle of a storm. The wind gripped the antenna as if to break it into little pieces. I hung on to the ladder with both arms. The metal was whistling as incredible winds played cat and mouse with the antenna. I wished for calmer weather on the ground. The strongest wind must have been at least 40 mph. Unfortunately, we couldn't communicate with Micke on the ground, and could only hope for the best.

As I passed the sixth cable, I had to scream for joy. We were now 990 feet above ground. The climb was over. I looked up to see if we could possibly get even higher, but the last 100 feet consisted of only a thin antenna. Well, 990 feet was more than enough. Scott, Bernard, and Herbert caught up with me and we crowded together on a small platform, no bigger than 10 square feet. Huddling on the platform, we took the opportunity to warm our hands on the hot warning lights which are always on to guide and warn airplane pilots. It felt painful but wonderful when the blood began circulating again through my frozen hands.

We prepared to jump. I checked my equipment. Was there enough slack between the pilot chute and the pin? Were my legstraps tight enough? Everything seemed okay. I asked Herbert to do a pin check. While the others were getting ready, I pulled a crumpled roll of toilet paper from my pocket. I rolled out a long piece and held it in my left hand. With my right hand I let go of the roll of paper, holding on to the piece in the left hand for a short while. The wind grabbed the paper with great force and within 30 seconds the roll had blown out of sight. The wind was strong, but at least it was blowing in the right direction, away from the antenna. I thought once more about how violent the landing could be if the wind was that strong at ground level.

Bernard asked me to hurry up for the second time since we started climbing. His face was blue and his teeth were chattering like the beat of a good rock-n-roll song. We all knew the seriousness of the moment. I closed my left hand around a metal strut. The pilot chute was in my right. I was standing on a projecting metal strut 990 feet above ground, ready to jump. The usual nasty weather of Skåne buffeted me with wind and rain. I looked down on the beautiful green fields and narrow gravel roads typical of the landscape in this part of the country. One last look at the other members of the Idiots' Club and off I went.

The moment I left my friends behind me, I felt an incredible calm come over me. This was the reward for the strenuous climb. I looked between my legs and saw how the antenna was rushing by. A quick, frightening look down. Two seconds, three seconds, four seconds…it felt like a whole minute. Cloudia opened up faithfully. I had fallen just over 265 feet.

I steered with the wind for a while and then turned up against the antenna at about 50 feet. I made a soft landing and luckily, the wind on the ground was no more than about 15 mph. Micke came running. I guess he was surprised that I came back in one piece. Before he could react, I kissed him on the mouth. I had my adrenaline kick, but he had not. Micke stared at me as if I had done something terrible.

I grabbed my canopy and concentrated on a small black spot high up on the antenna. Herbert. I was nervous. I had gotten Herbert into this in the first place and I hoped nothing bad would happen to him. Herbert was falling away from the antenna. He fell for three seconds before the canopy opened. He had made it. I could hear him scream for joy, "Yahoo! Yahoooo!"

He circled back and forth with his canopy, as if to show me how happy he was. Herbert made a nice, soft landing a few meters from where I stood. I ran up to him and we fell into each other's arms. He was so excited he could hardly get his words out. "Oh, Good Lord! I've never done anything like this. What a kick!"

But we could not call it a success yet. Scott and Bernard had yet to jump. It was Bernard's turn. He made a nice exit and fell for three seconds. When his canopy began to open I noticed something was wrong. The canopy was opening straight toward one of the cables and I held my breath, sure that he would collide. Happily, he flew a couple of feet below the cable, steering away from the antenna, screaming from relief and happiness. Luck was on his side this time. It was not difficult to figure out why the canopy had opened the way it did. Bernard had taken a great risk when he shoved the canopy into its container. He was lucky this time.

Scott jumped while Bernard was still in the air. He made a freefall of more than four seconds. The chute opened straight toward the antenna, just like Bernard's. Scott reacted immediately and quickly steered away from the antenna with the rear risers. Bernard, Herbert, and I ran to meet Scott and we rolled around for a while in the green summer grass. As always, it was wonderful to feel the great friendship which united us. We had successfully completed our third BASE jump together.

We walked to the woods where Micke had parked the car and opened the trunk. Before I stuffed in my canopy, I brought out some bottles of beer. There is nothing better than a beer after jumping from a TV antenna. We squeezed into the car and Micke gently pressed the accelerator and drove toward Lund. We were going to my parents' house.

As Micke drove at an even speed of 60 mph, Scott rolled down the back window. Bernard and I looked at each other knowingly. Scott was going to clown around, or should I say, do a stunt trick. He wiggled out of the back seat and onto the car roof. Micke didn't notice anything but kept driving unbeknownst of Scott's maneuver when he suddenly sat face to face with an ugly creature on the other side of the windshield. Scott was on the roof, pressing his face against the glass and making the ugliest faces he could muster. Micke didn't know what to do. For a while I wondered if Micke would panic and slam the breaks. Scott would fall down from the roof, get stuck between the tires and the asphalt, and end up as raw meat. I stretched my arm out through the window and pulled his pant leg, signaling it was time to come back inside. His feet came first, then the body. Finally, Bernard and I pulled him back in. Scott laughed his hearty laugh and looked at Micke, who didn't laugh at all.

I had called my brother Miki the night before the jump to tell him we were coming, and I knew my mother and Miki would be home in the morning. Miki had been given firm orders not to tell Mom. She had never before met Scott or Bernard. Dad had told her about my jump from Kochertalbrücke and the Montparnasse Tower. When I first heard this, I was irritated, but later realized that Dad had done me a favor. Mom was now prepared, and it would be easier to tell her about our next plan: Trollveggen. She has always been a very understanding and helpful mother, but it must have been a difficult period in her life; having a son who throws himself off buildings and bridges just for fun. Naturally, she must have worried that I would have to spend the rest of my life in a wheelchair.

I directed Micke to my parents' home in Lund. In the early 60s, sugar beets and wheat were grown here. Now the area is occupied by nine-story apartment buildings. In front of the apartments is a big, beautiful park; behind the buildings green hills serve as ski slopes in the winter for the people on the block. I remember sledding down the steepest part of the hill until the day I crashed straight into a tree. Our home was on the ninth floor in the middle apartment building. The view from the apartment was magnificent and in good weather one could see all the way to Copenhagen. On the street below was the school I attended through ninth grade. It was so close I could leave home when the bell rang and still make it on time for class.

We took the elevator to the ninth floor and I rang the doorbell. My mother opened the door inquisitively and her mouth fell open when she saw me. Before she could say anything, I stepped forward and gave her a hug. We had not seen each other in over six months.

"My little darling, what a surprise! You should have told me you were coming and I would have had breakfast ready for you."

My mother likes to take her time when she prepares a meal. Despite our surprise visit, she set to work enthusiastically. She asked if we were very hungry and all five of us answered, "YES!" We were starving after the strenuous climb up the antenna.

Miki awoke from what appeared to be a state of coma, struggled out of bed and met my friends. He looked like he had consumed a bottle of vodka the night before. His hair was standing on end, his eyes red and glossy. I grabbed his arm and led him to the living room where I told him a short version of our jump from the Hörby antenna. He shook his head and mumbled, "I have a crazy brother."

In the kitchen, my mother was busily preparing a royal breakfast. I didn't know how to begin to tell her about our jump, but upon reflection I chose the simple, direct style. "Mom, guess what? We just jumped off the Hörby antenna. Less than an hour ago."

I expected a violent reaction, but it didn't happen. In a calm voice she said, "But Jevto, are you telling me you jumped from that high antenna?"

I nodded. My mother began to laugh.

"Jevto, my son. You're nuts. But let's not talk any more about it. Help me with this tray, please. Breakfast is served."

Sorry, Mom—
Trollveggen is Next

We were sitting by the table when I told my mother about our next project, Trollveggen.

"Mom, I'm sorry but I can't stay very long today. Bernard and I are going to Norway this afternoon to jump from a cliff called Trollveggen."

I could tell she was thinking about the newspaper article she had sent me about the death of Carl Boenish. Poor Mom. She had set the breakfast table loaded with food and drink, just like when I lived at home. There were French rolls, juice, eggs, bacon, Kalle's caviar (Swedish fish roe in a toothpaste tube), cereal, hot chocolate, and Danish pastries. And there I was, her oldest son, informing her that I had just risked my life by jumping from a 990 feet high antenna. And that was not all. I went on to tell her I was now going to Norway to throw myself off a cliff. Mom remained very calm and I was proud of her. She reacted as if jumping from cliffs was a completely normal pastime. We remained at the table a long while, talking about BASE jumping in general, and the more we explained, the more interested she became. She also talked to Bernard and Scott and asked them how they liked Sweden. Bernard replied he had not seen very much of it yet, but that The Good Old Days restaurant and the Hörby antenna were well worth the visit.

Micke had relaxed now that the jump was over. He was enjoying a huge Danish roll which he dipped in hot chocolate before each bite. Herbert was in an excellent mood. A successful first BASE jump, an adrenaline rush, and a huge tasty breakfast; what else could you ask for?

The train for Norway departed from Copenhagen. We were planning to party before the train left and Miki was coming with us. I felt sad to leave Mom so soon, but we wanted to celebrate our jumps and had no time to spare. We said goodbye and I promised to call her as soon as Bernard and I had jumped from Trollveggen. Before she closed the door behind us, she whispered in my ear, "Jump carefully, sweetie-pie!"

Micke dropped us off at the Malmö harbor. Neither Herbert nor Micke wanted to party with us. I guess we were too crazy for them. We set our sights on a small bar by the Rådhusplats, a well-known plaza in Copenhagen. Scott knew the woman who owned the place from a few years back, and he assured us it was a bar with a great atmosphere. During the boat ride, Bernard had his first taste of good Danish beer and I purchased a bag of salt licorice, one of the few Swedish things I really missed in Paris. In Copenhagen, I looked up a Danish hot dog peddler. I bought four red hot dogs with buns on a paper plate. Ever since Sweden prohibited the use of the red food coloring used in these hot dogs, I would often go to Copenhagen to stuff myself with red hot dogs. I suppose I was drawn to the Stef Houlberg sausages because they were forbidden.

We walked along Ströget toward the Rådhusplats. Rådhuskroen, the bar where we were heading, was located on a narrow street by the Rådhusplats. It was a small, crowded British-style pub with thick wooden tables and wooden chairs. We sat down and began with a round of Carlsberg Gold. I noticed a poster by the door advertising an Irish band which would be playing all afternoon. Irish folk music in a small smoky bar is one of the things I most enjoy. A typical instrument is "the spoons." Scott, who is an accomplished spoon-player, explained how the instrument is handled. "Grip two table spoons with one hand, turn them with the rounded side toward each other and place one finger between them. Then, play along with the rhythm of the music." Or try to play along. It sounds simple, but in reality is very difficult and requires a lot of practice. We ordered round after round, alternating between Tuborg Black Gold and Carlsberg Gold.

The musicians arrived about 4 o'clock in the afternoon. They set up in a circle in the middle of the room. One of them, a short, bearded Irishman, pulled a tiny flute from his pocket and began playing. Soon other flutes, violins, and Irish drums were added and Bernard and I helped out by frantically drumming on the wooden table. Miki brought out his harmonica and played along as best he could. The atmosphere was fantastic. The rhythm of the Irish music made even the most laid-back guests in the bar stomp their feet. Unfortunately, Scott had to leave us after only a few hours to catch his flight to New York. We didn't know when we would meet again. He had landed a job as a salesman with the exclusive Cartier shop in New York and figured it could be his ticket into the jewelry world. I hugged Scott and we kissed goodbye on the cheeks.

After Scott's departure, the rest of us celebrated until nine that evening. The night-train to Norway was leaving at 10 o'clock. Miki, who was sufficiently drunk by this time, took the boat back to Malmö. The day had been so full of events and impressions that I had difficulty getting a clear picture of everything:

the jump from the antenna, breakfast with Mom, Copenhagen and the bar, Scott's departure, and our trip to Norway.

Trollveggen. Just the name gave me goose bumps. We were on our way to Oslo where we would transfer to a smaller local train to Åndalsnes. I had never been in Norway before, and looked forward to the visit. In Sweden, we tell jokes about the Norwegians, like Polack jokes in the States or jokes about Belgians in France. I thought it would be interesting to meet some real Norwegians and develop my own opinion about them. The train-ride was to last for eight hours, but we had not bothered to purchase tickets for a sleeping car. We reasoned that in our exhausted state, we would be able to sleep sitting up. We barely had sat down before both of us were sleeping soundly.

I awoke just as the train rolled into Oslo central station. We had two hours to pass before the train left for Åndalsnes. With our backpacks secured in a locker, we went out to explore the city. The first thing we noticed was the high price of beer. A bottle of beer was twice as much as in Denmark, and not only that; it was hard to find a store which sold beer. We walked around downtown Oslo for some time and when we got hungry we picked up bread, cheese, and a pint of milk in a convenience store. The Norwegian milk tasted wonderful, or maybe it was just that I had not tasted milk since I moved to Paris.

Bernard was not particularly impressed by the Norwegian capital. I wanted to show him the Kon-Tiki museum, but there was not enough time. Besides, we did not see a single pretty Norwegian lady, and this, of course, also had a negative impact on our mood.

The train ride to Åndalsnes took eight hours, so we had plenty of time to prepare ourselves mentally for our next BASE jump. I had a feeling that the jump from Trollveggen would be one of the most frightening in my short jumping career, but I didn't know why. I had heard about Trollveggen many times, usually in the form of disturbing newspaper headlines. "Two people seriously injured in jump from Trollveggen," or "Frenchman saved after 16 hours on ledge after unsuccessful Trollveggen jump." Despite all the accidents, Carl Boenish was the first person who had died as a result of jumping from Trollveggen. Two Germans had been seriously injured. One of them deployed his canopy much too late, while the other crashed into the cliff as the canopy opened. The Norwegian Air Force made a heroic effort navigating a rescue helicopter only a couple of feet from the cliff wall and pulling the Germans to safety. I understand they are both confined to wheelchairs today. I also knew of a Swedish jumper who broke his leg when his chute opened too close to the cliff. By the end of July 1984, a total of 84 people had jumped from Trollveggen. The cliff is mostly known for climbing.

It is 2000 feet high and vertical. Every year, dozens of climbers take on the challenge of climbing Trollveggen and many of them days on the mountain before they succeed.

I looked out the train window frequently during the ride and the view was breathtaking. The rail ran along a green valley, irrigated by the sky-blue Rauma river. Fishermen in waders fished for salmon in the middle of the river; the Romsdalen region of Norway is considered to be one of the world's best spots for salmon fishing. Bernard was also busy admiring the beauty of the Norwegian landscape. He asked me if I thought the mountains surrounding the valley looked frightening. I explained that the mere sight of a mountain gave me the creeps. I can't say I looked forward to jumping from Trollveggen at this point. It was only the desire to complete the project we had started, to become members of the BASE club, that pushed me forward. Both Bernard and I had completed the letters B, A, and S in the BASE acronym, and we were too close to achieving our goal to give up now.

Just before leaving Paris for our trip to Sweden and the Hörby antenna, I received a copy of Jean Boenish's newly published 20-page pamphlet about BASE jumping. It was entitled BASEics and covered most of the topics related to successfully leaping off a fixed object and living to tell the story. BASEics was the first comprehensive document published to help would-be BASE jumpers make their jumps as safe as possible. I was sitting in a Norwegian train, reading the advice a couple of hours before I was to leap off a sheer 2000-foot cliff. The first sentence of BASEics sounded more like a line from a Buddhist document than a guide book on how to skydive from buildings and cliffs:

> "BASE jumping is a unique and rewarding experience. It offers a natural combination of beauty, participation, and education that is not found in any other activity. In a 3 to 12-second freefall, a jumper can discover the personality of an object on its own terms. To instantly experience a huge object gives new perspective to its relationship to man & a more intimate respect and enjoyment of existence on a grander scale."

In BASEics Jean Boenish covered everything from selecting the appropriate fixed object to jump from, to the preparation for the jump as well as selecting the right gear. The procedures for the jump itself were covered on two pages, including the following nugget:

"**Procedure 5:** If the jumper has unwittingly let go of his standard hand-held pilot chute on exit, it usually bobbles above his back until about the third second, when there is enough air speed to snatch the pilot chute away."

This is exactly what happened when Scott made his first leap from the Montparnasse Tower. Five small words had saved Scott's life: "until about the third second." Had it been "until about the forth second," he would have been dead as a doornail. When I had finished reading BASEics, I summed up the contents for Bernard in this way: "Since the beginning of our BASE adventure together we have done the contrary of most of what Jean Boenish recommends in BASEics and incredibly we are still alive. I just hope our luck will stay with us until after the jump from Trollveggen" I finished by reading the last lines aloud:

"Each BASE object presents its jumper with a unique view which imparts an intimate and poignant experience of that object. From exit through the first second of freefall, the jumper takes in the surroundings of the object. Then, towards the 2nd second of fall, gravity pulls the jumper from the head-high position into a prone position. There, in the silence of a new time frame, the jumper watches as the object picks up speed, and the jumper is thrown back into the immediate sense of time of a standard skydive. The object rushes by, the jumper moves off, and the intimacy of the jump fades away. When the canopy opens, the process stops, and the jumper is pulled back into normality. The size of the object is put back into perspective, and the jumper descends back down to the ground. But the experience will always exist for the jumper to recall, relive, and learn from."

The train puffed along through Romsdalen. The combination train engineer/tourist guide provided a running commentary about our surroundings over the loudspeaker, making us laugh uncontrollably. "Hello, hello! This is your train engineer speaking. We will soon pass the small village, Hamsfjorn, which you will see on your right. The village is mostly known for its beautiful stave church." A few minutes later, he was back on the loudspeaker. "Hello, hello! A few minutes ago I told you we would soon pass Hamsfjord village on your right, and we are now passing that village on your right."

Bernard folded over double from laughter. The engineer continued to entertain us in this manner all the way to Åndalsnes.

"Hello, hello! You can now see the famous cliff Trollveggen, Europe's highest vertical cliff, on your left. It is mainly known for its connection with the reckless climbers who tackle the difficult climb every year. During the last few years, it has also become a popular jump site for skydivers."

Bernard and I stared out the window curiously. This was Trollveggen? It didn't look particularly high. To reassure both Bernard and myself, I told him to consider our distance from the cliff. It is difficult to judge the height of anything from a great distance. I would have guessed the height to be no more than 1000 feet. It was grayish-black in color and I spotted snow in some places.

The train rolled into Åndalsnes station shortly after three in the afternoon. The train station was very small and looked a lot like a station in the picturesque region of Småland (Sweden), with all the buildings painted the same red color. We found a telephone booth and called a man by the name of Ronald Ytterli. Ronald had been Scott's and Christophe's guide to Trollveggen when they made their jumps. He worked as a fireman in the Åndalsnes area. I dialed the four-digit number and waited for him to answer. After two rings, I heard a deep male voice on the other end.

I introduced myself and told him why we were in the neighborhood. Ronald explained in easy-to-understand Norwegian that he was glad we had contacted him and it would be an honor to guide us to Trollveggen. He gave us directions to his parents' house, close to the railroad station. Bernard and I grabbed our backpacks and walked down a paved street leading to a residential area. The homes were well-kept, the lawns trimmed, and the gravel walkways raked.

Ronald's parents' house was an average sized yellow brick house, surrounded by a lawn. I rang the doorbell impatiently. A big, tall, muscular young man opened the door and invited us in. Ronald was blond with blue eyes. We sat down on a comfortable couch in the living room, where he immediately took charge.

"Okay, so you are friends of Scott's and that weird Frenchman. If I recall correctly, they each made three jumps from Bruraskaret. Scott sure liked to party. The only things he was interested in after jumping were beer and pretty Norwegian women. The problem is that there is neither in Åndalsnes." He continued, "Today is the first decent day in three weeks. You should try to jump tonight. Don't miss this chance." He told us that a group of Swedish jumpers had been waiting for good weather for more than two weeks, only to give up a few days ago and return home.

My body immediately reacted to what Ronald said. My hands turned wet with sweat and my stomach protested with a rumble. I had looked forward to a quiet evening with plenty of time to prepare myself mentally. Now I was expected to make an immediate decision. Bernard and I discussed what to do and agreed to attempt a jump that same day. We pulled the chutes from our backpacks and spread them out on the lawn behind the house. This would be the most important packing of my life. I talked to myself as I packed, "Jevto, this will be a tough jump, but try to stay calm and everything will be fine."

It was more important than ever that Cloudia open properly. My main concern was twisted lines. During jumps from airplanes there is plenty of time to untwist the lines. This would not be the case during our jump from Trollveggen. We planned to freefall for six to eight seconds: three seconds of acceleration and five seconds tracking. As I mentioned earlier, the tracking position is used during skydives to achieve a horizontal separation from other jumpers. This time, it would be used to get as far away as possible from the cliff.

As we reached the last phase of packing, we paused for the drawing. Bernard had a Norwegian coin which he hid in one hand behind his back. The person who picked the hand with the coin would be the first to jump. I happened to point to the empty hand. I had lost again.

Ronald encouraged us to hurry up. It was getting late. I changed into my favorite jeans, a pair of 501s, a sweatsuit jacket, and headband. A friend of Ronald's, Svein Brevik, was going to accompany us to the jump site, Bruraskaret. He drove a rusty Ford Fiesta which was parked on the street by the house. We placed our parachutes in the trunk and sat down in the back seat. Ronald looked like a genuine mountain guide in his *lederhosen* (knee-length pants) and heavy walking boots. He carried a small backpack with bottled water and rusks. Svein took the driver's seat and prepared his old Fiesta for an exhausting drive. We headed for a cabin called Trollstigen, high in the mountains. This cabin was owned by Ronald's parents and served as a starting point for treks in the beautiful mountains. It was open only during the tourist season, four months a year. The rest of the year, Ronald's parents lived off the income from the tourist season. The road wound its way up the mountain. Ronald explained the Åndalsnes community spends millions of *kroner* each year for repairs of frost-damaged roads. The Fiesta huffed and puffed in second gear. First gear was out of commission.

Arriving at Trollstigen, we went inside to meet Ronald's parents. His mother was busy serving food to several hungry young men. We introduced ourselves and she inquired whether we were skydivers. Ronald told her we had just arrived and were about to make our first jump from Bruraskaret. She was kind enough to prepare a small packet with a bottle of juice and a bun for us. We did not stay long in the cabin as we had a long walk ahead of us. Ronald's mother wished us good luck and we felt we needed it badly.

Bernard and I attached our parachutes and were barely finished when Ronald and Svein took off in a hurry. I had never seen human mountain goats until I saw the two of them run up the steep path, exerting no more effort than on a leisurely

Sunday walk. Bernard and I started off in the same tempo, but soon began to lag behind. While Ronald took two steps, I barely managed one. The sun was beating down, but the temperature was only 50 degrees in the shade.

After walking for a little over an hour, we arrived at an orange metal sign erected by the police. It was fastened to the ground with two sturdy metal poles. In big black letters it read, verbatim, "**WARNING**. Due to narrow ravine and unpredictable winds in the mountainside, cliff-jumping (parachuting) in Trollveggen has proven hazardous. If accident demands rescue assistance at public expense, national authorities will sue for compensation." It was signed "The Police" with the f-word in front of it, penciled in by some clown. Bernard noticed my worried expression when I read the sign and said it was a good thing he did not understand English.

We continued our trek up the mountain. The groundcover shifted from rocks to snow. I sank through the frozen crust as I struggled along. My feet were soon frozen and felt like two heavy blocks of ice. Ronald and Svein kept up the high speed and, amazingly, were not even short of breath. My tongue protruded from my mouth, I was panting, and I felt like I had used up most of my strength. We had climbed, walked, and jumped along the steep path for more than two-and-a-half hours. My physical exhaustion slowly but surely developed into mental anguish. According to Ronald, we had less than half an hour walk left.

The thought of jumping from a 2000-foot-high cliff made me sick. How nice it would have been to stretch out on a white sandy beach with a glass of ice-cold beer. To let the soft sand run between my fingers as a beautiful woman gently rubbed my back. Instead, I was perspiring heavily, climbing up a mountain with a parachute just so I could throw myself off a cliff. "Jevto, take it easy. Concentrate. You will soon make an important decision. You are going to jump from a cliff." Seconds later, my thoughts took a different direction. "Jevto, pay attention! What are you doing in Åndalsnes? You're not going to jump from that dangerous Trollveggen, are you? Think about what you're doing!" Despite these thoughts it was difficult to imagine us turning back and walking down the same path again. I knew we would both jump and that's what frightened me.

Ronald dashed along ahead of us. We followed a narrow path, winding itself between huge boulders. The pain in my feet was excruciating and was not made better by having to jump from boulder to boulder with Cloudia on my back. Suddenly, Ronald stopped about 30 feet in front of me.

"This is it!" he yelled.

I looked in Ronald's direction and saw the earth abruptly end in front of him. The boulders around us were dark gray and terrifying. The humidity was high and the wind ice-cold. I slowly walked up to the steep drop-off. The view was magnificent and at the same time frightening. Had I been a normal tourist, I would have admired the breathtaking landscape 2000 feet below for a long time. But in this self-inflicted situation, the mountain and the drop-off made me shiver. Did I really have to jump from here? I turned toward Bernard and found him standing in the spot where I had been a few minutes earlier. He refused to come forward to have a look. He was too afraid. He asked if it looked bad and I gave him a serious nod in reply. We finished the last preparations for the jump. Normally, my chute hangs comfortably on my body, but this time I was suddenly afraid it would come lose during the freefall and I secured it tightly.

Another jumper had painted the words, "600 meters until impact" in white letters on a rock just by the launch site. This was not an encouraging message.

I had heard about the ritual of the mandatory signature in the green book. Hidden in a cleft is a metal box which contains a small notebook and a pen, a guest book of sorts. You are supposed to fill out name, nationality, jump number, and perhaps a quick remark if so inclined. I flipped the pages in the notebook and came upon a few funny notes like, "Bye Mother, I love you" and "They told me there was an elevator down!"

Bernard's number was TV85 and mine TV86 (TV as in Trollveggen). Number 83 and 84 belonged to two Germans who had jumped the previous day. I would be the 86th person to jump from Trollveggen.

The sun was setting on the horizon and it was getting dark. We did not have much time. Jumping in the dark would be too dangerous. Before I jumped, I wanted to taste the bun Ronald's mother had given me. If I was going to die, it was not going to happen on an empty stomach. I finished the bun and rinsed it down with a swallow of juice. It had barely reached my stomach before it came up again. The vomit splashed on the rock in front of me: the entire bun, the juice, and a little bile. Ronald's and Svein's eyes grew big as they watched me. I believe they presumed it was part of my concentration tactic. They took their positions with the camera, 15 feet to the right of the exit point.

We were ready to jump. Bernard, who was to jump first, stood on the tiny platform leading into nothingness. He looked tense. I held my breath. Bernard looked to the sky, then turned toward me and yelled the Idiot's Club motto as he made a powerful leap ahead. I quickly leaned over the edge but could not see him. Suddenly Ronald yelled, "He crashed into the cliff!"

Bernard was dead. I was certain his canopy had opened facing the wall and he had been crushed to death against the sharp rocks. Scott had been lucky when he survived the crash into the Montparnasse Tower. Trollveggen was less forgiving.

It went so fast. Ten seconds ago Bernard was standing with me on top of the mountain and now he was dead. Gone forever.

Despite the loss, I was determined to jump. I saw no reason not to. Bernard would have been angry with me if he knew I had walked all the way down because of him. I positioned myself on the ledge, prepared to jump. My head felt completely empty. My best friend had died during his fourth BASE jump. My mother was right. Trollveggen was a death trap.

Just as suddenly as he had died, Bernard came to life again. "There he is!" yelled Ronald. I peeked over the edge and caught sight of his blue canopy slowly moving away from the mountain wall. Bernard was alive. Exhilarated, I prepared to jump. I checked my equipment one last time. Everything appeared to be in order. Three feet from the edge, I tried to find a good spot to place my feet. A running exit was out of the question since the ledge was less than six feet deep. I looked down at the beautiful valley below, then up to the sky and the light pink clouds. This was it.

I made my upper body sway back and forth. "Now! No, not yet. Now! No, I'll count to ten…six, seven, eight, nine, ten." I pushed away from the ledge and left that forbidding mountain once and for all. As I began my fall along the bare cliff wall I counted aloud. At three, I took the tracking position. I could see the gray mountain rush by at a great speed from the corner of my eye. Five. Six. Two more seconds. I started to think it was almost time to deploy the chute. Seven. Eight. I grabbed the pilot chute and threw it at the same time as I prayed to my personal God that Cloudia would open as usual. Boom! Cloudia opened with a powerful bang. I lifted my head to make sure everything was in order above me. I gave out a happy scream when I realized the canopy was intact and fit for landing. I felt like a fly who just escaped the fly swatter.

The small landing site was far, far below, close to the river. The grassy area were I was to land was only 80 feet square. It was a fantastic feeling to fly between the high mountains. Without a sound, I sailed through the beautiful landscape like a bird of prey. It was very difficult to judge the height above ground as it slanted at about the same degree as the canopy's angle of descent. I caught sight of the landing area after Bernard had already landed and was gathering his blue canopy. I dropped some altitude by turning steeply a couple of times above the landing site. At 160 feet I steered toward the middle of the grassy area and then landed softly.

As my feet touched the ground I almost shed some tears of joy. Bernard came running toward me and threw himself in my arms for a powerful bear hug. The first thing he said was, "Let's not jump again. Ever."

I agreed completely. "Never again!"

Looking up at Bruraskaret, I studied the place, 2000 feet above me, where we had stood only three minutes earlier. I thought to myself it would not be possible to reach any higher anxiety levels than what I experienced on top of that mountain. The jump from Trollveggen was the most nerve-racking thing I had ever done, but also the most exciting. The adrenaline rush lasted for hours afterward.

I picked up my canopy and walked with one arm around Bernard's shoulders toward the road leading back to Åndalsnes. As we walked, Bernard explained what happened when he released his pilot chute. The freefall went as planned, but the canopy deployed dangerously close to the mountain wall. It is always difficult to estimate the distance toward a flat wall, but Bernard insisted that he had been about 30 feet from the it. He made a 180-degree turn and steered away from the wall, and this was when Ronald spotted him. Most likely, Bernard didn't track enough, not leaving enough space between himself and the wall before the canopy deployed.

We managed to stop a car on its way to Åndalsnes. The Norwegian driver got fired up when we told him about the jump, and wanted to hear our story again and again during the 20 minute drive. He dropped us off by Ronald's parents' house and we narrowly escaped having to sign autographs.

We were surprised to find two pretty girls waiting for us at Ronald's house, both pink-cheeked and blonde. We assumed they were girlfriends of Ronald and Svein. My only wish was to sit down on a comfortable couch with a cold beer. My adrenaline-pumped body needed rest. It was pitch black outside and there was no sign of either Ronald nor Svein. I wasn't too worried; they had grown up in the area and could probably find their way home even in the worst snowstorm. Sure enough, a few minutes later they appeared, jogging into the yard. They had run down the mountain and were not even out of breath. True men of steel. They were happy to see us alive and congratulated us on our first Trollveggen jump. Bernard and I went outside to pitch our tent. We had permission to spend our first night in Åndalsnes in Ronald's yard. With tremendous effort we managed to pitch the tent, using the last of our strength.

Despite mental and physical exhaustion we wanted to check out the village's hotspot, the discotheque Bellevue. Bernard found the French name a funny choice for a discotheque in a tiny village which looked more like the end of the world than anything else. Bellevue turned out to be like any big-city discotheque. The music pulsated from the big speakers and the village's in-crowd did everything to maintain an exhilarating atmosphere. We sat down and ordered two beers.

Within half an hour, we were famous. Ronald had spread the word about our jumps among his friends and the evening belonged to us. I would have spent all night dancing with the cute Norwegian girls, had I only been in better shape. My eyelids felt heavy and Bernard's tongue protruded from his mouth. The prettier the Norwegian girl, the more it protruded.

After a short but intensive visit at the nightclub, we headed toward our tent. We couldn't wait to get some sleep. Walking toward the tent, Bernard confessed that he had cheated. He had been so terrified to have to jump last, that he had fixed the drawing in his favor. He had moved the coin to his other hand when I, in reality, had won. When I finally crawled into my sleeping bag and closed my eyes, I felt total relief. We had made our jumps from Trollveggen and survived. We never had to jump from the frightening wall again.

Base 66

Bernard and I spent three days in Åndalsnes. Every morning before breakfast we swam in the ice-cold river outside the village. Our days were spent hiking in the mountains. By the second day we already felt like we knew all the villagers; everybody greeted us wherever we went. I don't know if this was because they recognized us as the "jumpers" or if this was just their natural behavior, saying hello to everybody.

The weather was very bad during our three days of vacation, which in a way was a good thing. We didn't feel pressured to make another jump. Before we boarded the train to Paris, I wrote a postcard to my mother, telling her we had both jumped from Trollveggen and everything had gone well.

Back in my small room in Paris, I wrote a letter to Carl Boenish's widow Jean, where I applied for our BASE jumper numbers on behalf of Scott, Bernard, and myself. I described the four jumps: Kochertalbrücke (S), The Montparnasse Tower (B), the Hörby antenna (A), and Trollveggen (E), and enclosed a few photos. I also included dates, heights of the objects and their geographical locations. Almost four months later, on October 25, 1984, I received a letter from Jean:

> Dear Jevto,
>
> Please excuse the long delay in my response. Congratulations! You are BASE 66 and Bernard Poirrier is BASE 65. From the information I have, there are now 16 Europeans with BASE, you being the latest. It is probably safe to say that you are the first Swede and Bernard the first Gaul (Frenchman). Bridge Day went very well; 248 jumpers made 563 jumps in 6 hours. I'm glad there were not too many jumpers; hopefully we will have about the same number next year, and see you there too.
>
> Sincerely,
> Jean Boenish

She enclosed three embroidered BASE logos to fasten on our jacket sleeves. The logo showed a person freefalling between a building, an antenna, a cliff, and a bridge with the words "BASE JUMPER" spelled out in a circle around the picture. As membership in the BASE club had been our main purpose, the BASE logo was proof that we had reached our goal. We were members of a club in which only 66 people in the world had gained entry. And I was the last member.

I left my job at Facit at the end of July and returned to Sweden. An idea had taken hold in my mind: I would try to make some money by selling the story about our BASE jumps to the Swedish press. The first newspaper I contacted was *Kvällsposten.* They sent a journalist to meet with me and two days later a two-page article appeared in the Saturday edition. The style of the article was quite sensationalist. The headline read: "YES, WE ARE NUTS!" The first few lines included an attempt to introduce us. "Jevto Dedijer flings his blonde hair away from his eyes and smiles boyishly. Jevto is the first Swedish person to become a so-called BASE jumper. He is one of only 16 such audacious persons in all of Europe." The journalist described the four BASE jumps and concluded: "They are joined in a fellowship where death is the opponent. Jevto laughs out loud: 'We are nuts!'"

A photo of the Montparnasse Tower covered a full page. It had the typical dotted line from the top of the tower to the street below. "This is where it happened!"

After reading the *Kvällsposten* article a couple of times I realized that the journalist was not interested in what I had accomplished, but only in how to make the article as dramatic as possible to sell more newspapers. My attitude toward the news media and the press in particular had been idealistic and naive. I had assumed journalists would be interested in the story, and attempt to learn more about the subject.

Before the next interview, I decided to try to sway the journalist to write about how I experienced my BASE jumps and avoid rushing ahead with home-made interpretations and expressions.

The next article appeared in the men's journal *Lektyr.* I hesitated when they called to set up a time and place for an interview. I had read a few copies of the magazine and was not sure I wanted to appear with my name and picture in a men's magazine. After a short time of consideration, I decided to accept. By this time, I had learned to charge for the interviews and most important, not to say a word until the reporter had agreed to the amount I requested. This could take a long time and many times the reporters had to call their editors for permission. I felt cheated by the reporter from *Kvällsposten* and did not want to be cheated again. The two journalists from *Lektyr* readily agreed to pay what I requested.

The *Lektyr* article turned out very well. It included two four-color spreads and was very well written. As always, it had a bold headline and powerful introduction. "ONE MISTAKE MEANS DEATH!" it read, followed by a dramatic statement. "With only 300 meters to the ground, Jevto Dedijer leaps off the Hörby antenna in Skåne. Everything must fall into place during the jump—or Jevto will die!" The only thing I objected to was a photo of me holding a bottle of champagne. "Jevto Dedijer, 21, celebrates with champagne after four successful BASE jumps." The reporter had brought the bottle from Stockholm for the sole purpose of taking this photo. When they left, they took the bottle with them. I didn't get to taste a single drop.

One evening, a journalist from the newspaper *Arbetet* called, wondering if I would comment on a fatal jump from Trollveggen. He explained that a 19-year-old Swede had been crushed to death in a jump from Trollveggen, and he wanted my opinion. I refused to comment on the young man's death, but chose to tell him about my own experiences. The following day, the paper published a two-page article about the fatal jump along with my comments. "JEVTO TELLS WHY HE PLAYS WITH DEATH! Rules are made to be broken," says 22-year-old Jevto Dedijer of Lund. "I don't encourage BASE jumping, but I never say no if someone asks my advice." Next to the article with my comments was a big picture of Trollveggen with an arrow. The text read: "This is where Jörgen, 19, fell to his death!" The newspaper had acquired a photo of Jörgen and the article continued: "The Trollveggen adventure ended in 19-year-old Jörgen Håkansson's death…"

The same news was treated more dramatically by the evening newspaper *Expressen*. "HE WATCHED HIS FRIEND FALL TO HIS DEATH," read the headline. Like *Arbetet*, they showed a photo of Trollveggen with a dotted line indicating the fall. "Jörgen Håkansson's parachute did not open. He fell uncontrollably and was crushed against the rocks. Then he rolled over a cliff ledge and fell another 700 meters." I sympathized with Jörgen's parents and family who had to read about his death described in horrifying and often humiliating detail by every newspaper in Sweden.

After the fatal accident, my friends asked me how I survived my jump from Trollveggen and if I planned to jump there again. The strange thing with all terrible accidents is that people actually enjoy reading about them. I don't mean to imply that this is strange behavior, but rather a human behavior. We thrive on other people's misery. When a skydiver is killed in a jump, something paradoxical happens. The number of students in jump courses increases. One might think a fatal accident would deter people from skydiving, but the opposite is true. The sport gains interest.

A few weeks after Jörgen Håkansson's death, a Finnish jumper was killed in a jump from Trollveggen. Three months later, another fatal accident. "THE DEATH CLIFF CLAIMS ITS FOURTH VICTIM," wrote Kvällsposten. "Norway's death cliff, the dangerous 5000 feet (!?) vertical Trollveggen claimed its fourth victim yesterday." If the journalists could have used only adjectives in their articles, I am certain they would have.

What was remarkable was the fact that more than 200 jumps had been made from Trollveggen during a period of five years without a single fatal accident—and suddenly there were four fatalities in a row. Perhaps the reason could be found in jumpers underestimating the degree of difficulty of the site.

Jumping Across the Atlantic

I could support myself for a few weeks on the money I earned from an interview, but the income was very sporadic. I took a job as a substitute teacher in English and French in Lund and saved up enough money for a trip to the United States to visit Scott. It had been a year since Bernard, Scott, and I had seen each other. We agreed to meet at Scott's place in Stamford, Connecticut, not far from New York City. The purpose of the trip was to visit the New River Gorge Bridge, one of the world's highest bridges with a 876-foot drop. For the past few years, Jean Boenish had been in charge of arranging jumps from the bridge on the second Saturday of October. We thought it would be a good idea to combine our get-together with one or two BASE jumps.

Before the trip, Scott sent me a picture of a "Basemobile" he had rented for the 12 hour drive to the bridge. The photo showed a camper with five beds, shower, stove, refrigerator, stereo and a television set. He wrote in his letter he planned to fill the refrigerator with food and purchase a 16-gallon keg of beer.

We met at the home of Scott's mother two days before the jump. The first evening together we partied like never before. We were sincerely happy to be back together. The drive to the New River Bridge went quickly and painlessly. This was the first time I traveled in a camper. Comfortable on one of the beds with a book and a beer, I quickly forgot I was on the road.

We arrived at the bridge at 4 a.m. and got three hours of sleep before roll call. After a good breakfast in the Basemobile, we stepped out to meet the other jumpers and to my great surprise, there were more than 250 of us. Everybody was to jump between 9 a.m. and 4 p.m. It was absolutely forbidden to jump at any other time. BASE jumping is an important part of a big yearly celebration acknowledging the construction of the bridge. People come from near and far to party and watch crazy people jump from the bridge. Jean Boenish was in charge of organizing the jumps and informed the participants of the water level (the landing site was a sandbank in the river below), security details, and equipment. For many of the participants, this was their first BASE jump and she especially emphasized body position during exit. I took the opportunity to talk to some of the other

BASE jumpers about their experiences. Phil Smith, who had made 150 BASE jumps at the time, supplied me with many good tips.

A crowd of 150,000 people was already waiting on the bridge before 9 a.m. and we almost had to push our way through. As always in the United States, most everything was provided for. Hot dog stands, pizza stands, milk shake bar, souvenir shops, candy vendors…and much more. I stood in the middle of a winding line of people, feeling like I was waiting in line at the post office instead of waiting to jump from a bridge. After more than two hours, my turn had come. I wore a pair of shorts in a pretty strawberry pattern and a colorful T-shirt. A woman selling candy approached me just as I was getting in position to jump, offering her goods. I politely declined. Somebody in the crowd helped me get on top of the bridge rail. I noticed a cameraman about ten feet above me, filming the jumps from a comfortable crane basket, the type of crane used by firemen for rescue purposes. He was in a position to get excellent shots of all the jumps.

I looked into the camera, yelled, "Long live Sweden!" and jumped. Cloudia opened after a freefall of four seconds, quickly and perfectly. I soon realized I would not make it to the sandy area designated as the landing site, and instead made a soft landing at the edge of the waterline. The landing site was very small due to the high water level. The surrounding area was full of what looked like tiny rocks from the air, but turned out to be good-sized boulders. Several jumpers misjudged the size of the rocks and suffered broken legs or ankles. Scott and Bernard jumped together a few seconds after me and landed on the sandbank.

After landing, I looked up at the bridge. What is great about the New River Bridge is that one can watch hundreds of BASE jumps in a single day. Eventually, it actually became boring. Below the bridge, three fast motor boats waited in the water to pick up jumpers who landed in the middle of the river and risked being pulled down with their chutes.

I let Cloudia air-dry in the cool October breeze and then packed her up for a second jump. Reaching the top of the bridge, we noticed most people had chosen to make only one jump. There was no line-up. Scott and Bernard jumped holding hands. They let go of each other after two seconds and their chutes opened normally. My second jump resembled my first, except that I allowed myself to joke with the audience before I took off. Behind me was a young girl with her mother. I looked at the little girl seriously and asked if she wanted to join me in a jump. The poor girl shook her head and looked at me with frightened eyes. Her young mother played along and encouraged her daughter to go with me. Just before she was about to panic, I quit the game and patted her head reassuringly. I left the audience behind with a powerful jump for a few seconds of exhilaration.

In the evening, all the jumpers gathered at a hotel to watch videos of the jumps. Six hundred fifty jumps had been made during the day, with the worst consequences being a few broken ankles. I don't believe I have ever met so many nutcases in one place before. All the people your mother warned you against when you were little were gathered there. It was fun to be able to talk BASE jumping with anybody and be understood and respected immediately. Everybody had the same ideas about BASE jumping and life in general.

The most fascinating thing about the New River jumps was the atmosphere. At the time, the New River site was one of very few places in the world where people could gather and skydive from a bridge without the risk of being caught. It all seemed so natural that some of the excitement actually disappeared. In all honesty, I must admit that I prefer jumps which include a little mystery and without a crowd of 150,000, souvenir shops, and concession stands. Still, Bernard, Scott, and I had a great time together. We slept one night in our camper and early the next morning we headed toward New York. I had purchased a weekend ticket and had to return to Lund.

Back to the City of Lights

After my return to Lund I began working as a night clerk at Grand Hotel. It was a boring job, with very little customer contact. When I began my shift at 11 p.m., the guests were about to go to bed and my duties included making sure the hotel did not burn down and that the guests could sleep undisturbed. After a little more than a year at Grand Hotel, I decided to return to France. I had good memories from my time in Paris and enjoyed the French lifestyle.

One morning, while reading the *SydSvenskan* newspaper, my eye caught an employment ad that appealed to me. "Swedish organizer of bus trips seeks hotel manager for newly built hotel in Paris." I sent my references to the travel agency and was called in for an initial interview. It went well and a week later I was called for a second interview. I was very nervous both times, almost as nervous as before a BASE jump. I tried to relax by telling myself, "Jevto, if you can handle a jump from Trollveggen, you can certainly handle a job interview."

It helped a little. The president of the agency called a week after my second interview wondering if I still was interested in the position. Just like that I had become the manager of a hotel. This brought on great anxiety and I wondered what I had gotten myself into. Would I be able to run a hotel in Paris after only a year's experience as a receptionist? "This won't do. I need to keep my cool and go for it," I thought. "If I keep questioning myself I'll never make it!"

After two weeks training in Malmö, I was sent off to Paris. The first time I saw my hotel I was stunned. In place of an entry door there were two thick wooden planks with a chain and a padlock. A huge turning cement mixer occupied the reception area. The six-story hotel was a total mess, lacking things like wallpaper, carpet, and furniture. The only thing I knew for sure was that guests would arrive in 12 weeks.

Where could I purchase butter, bread, and jam for the hotel breakfasts? Who would deliver the bottles for the mini-bars in the hotel rooms? How would I go about hiring cleaning staff? What type of marble floor should go in the reception area? Which bakery had the best croissants? I stayed awake at night wondering how to solve all my problems. I hired cleaning ladies from Portugal, night receptionists from Algeria, and front desk staff from Denmark. The hiring process completed, I began training the new employees at the same time as I studied accounting. It was my job to keep track of the hotel's finances, and as I had never before dealt with amounts in the millions, I had to study hard.

The first guests arrived February 17, 1987, and unfortunately did not have the best of stays. The mini-bars were still empty due to delivery delays and the television sets did not work because the satellite dish on the roof was not yet installed. When the guests called the front desk to order a cup of coffee I would send personnel to the closest café on the block to buy it. The coffee machine in the breakfast room was out of order.

After an initial period of about a month, all the machines in the hotel were finally in working order, but other problems arose. The winter had been unusually cold and as the snow melted, part of the snowmelt disappeared from the roof straight into the hotel. The paint in the stairwell peeled and landed on the carpet and the hotel guests like huge snowflakes. The problem was taken care of by a painting business and immediately another problem came up. A water pump in the basement quit working. Normally, water from the toilets on the bottom two floors would collect in a sump two levels below ground, near the breakfast room. From there, the water was pumped 20 feet up and out into the sewer. When the pump quit working, the sump filled up first, then the hallway in front of the dining area, and finally the dining room itself was taking in water. Obviously, this was not exactly clean water, and it smelled horrible. I realized I had a problem when the hotel guests asked if I was raising pigs in the hotel. I knew I had to do something when the neighbors complained about a foul odor covering the entire block. A specially equipped tank truck drained the water with the help of a wide pipe. Several plumbers were hired and quickly replaced the worn-out pump.

I worked seven days a week, 12 hours a day, during my first year as a hotel manager. My office, which was barely big enough to hold an Ikea desk, was 13 feet below ground and without windows. I was not able to stand upright in my office and rarely invited visitors to my "hole in the ground." Despite the problems I encountered, the hotel ran satisfactorily. The staff consisted of hard-working people and I was happy to have succeeded in creating a nice atmosphere. My few visitors from Sweden told me I resembled John Cleese of the TV show *Fawlty Towers*. I had to admit I was proud to hear it. I have always dreamed of having a beer with John Cleese at a London pub some day.

One Sunday afternoon I was invited for tea at the home of a French lady I had come to know through Scott. Her home was located in the affluent seventh arrondissement in Paris. The guests were all very spiffy dressers and, I am sorry to say, very boring. Inadvertently, I addressed a young man of about 25 inappropriately, and when I also mentioned that I neither hunted nor lived in a castle, he turned away to converse with someone of his own kind.

I was prepared to leave after an hour and three cups of tea when I spotted a slim, petite, dark-haired woman. She did not appear as stuck-up as the other guests. I offered her a cup of Earl Grey tea and introduced myself. She had to repeat her name three times before I caught on: Yolaine de Saint Just d'Autingues. We talked for hours and before we left I asked her for her phone number. I noted it carefully in my address book. Her simple, direct manner and sense of humor had appealed to me.

Yolaine and I had dinner two weeks after our first meeting over the Earl Grey. We enjoyed each other's company so much that I eventually left my apartment and moved in with Yolaine. For the first time since I began my management career, I worked less than 12 hours a day. I was in love for the first time in my life and it was a fantastic feeling. Yolaine read poetry to me and taught me French history and culture.

Yolaine and I were married after one year. The wedding took place at her aunt's castle, Château de Gambais, just outside Paris. I remember well how Yolaine's father apologetically explained he could not organize a big wedding. A small wedding is better than no wedding, I thought. I could not believe my ears when he told me he had invited *only* 250 guests. Twenty of my best Swedish friends joined us for the wedding dinner at Château de Gambais. As the dinner was coming to an end and the dance was to begin, a friend approached me and whispered, "Jevto, this is better than *Dallas.*" (The TV-series, that is.)

From the adrenaline-generating adventures with Scott and Bernard, I was now entering a new kind of adventure with Yolaine.

After six months of marriage, Yolaine reassured me of her love by skydiving for the first time. Yolaine was strapped to my good friend Anders Thulin in a tandem jump. Anders had more than 1,500 skydives under his belt at the time. Yolaine and Anders jumped from 13,000 feet, closely followed by me. I linked with Yolaine during the freefall and gave her a kiss on the lips at 120 miles per hour. We held hands for 60 seconds as we fell toward Mother Earth. Yolaine and Anders landed softly under the same canopy and her first skydive was a success.

The Idiots' Club Today

BASE jumping organizations have sprung up in countries around the world. The initial pioneering spirit has disappeared, for better or worse. Some people even BASE jump full-time for a living (often not for long). Today, there are companies which manufacture equipment solely for BASE jumping, such as specially made canopies, containers, pilot chutes, and all kinds of accessories. As the equipment has become more advanced, it has become possible to jump from lower altitudes. Not too long ago, I read about an Englishman who jumped from the Notre Dame Cathedral in Paris, and jumps are being made regularly from a 165-foot-high bridge above the St. Lawrence River in Quebec City. Still, the sport is mainly practiced by a handful of adventurous souls. As of this writing, only 900 people worldwide have completed the 4 jumps needed to earn their own Base jumper numbers. Compare this to the 404 astronauts who have visited space through the years, or the 1,900 people who have climbed Mount Everest.

The internet has also been a very helpful tool for the relatively small BASE jumping community. There are numerous websites specialized in making it as easy as possible to get into BASE jumping. Nick Di Giovanni, BASE 194, maintains and regularly updates the "World BASE Fatality List" on the web. On October 5, 2004 an experienced BASE jumper with over 1200 jumps died while jumping from the JinMao Tower in Shanghai. He deployed with line twists and hit a rooftop on an adjacent structure. He became the 82nd BASE fatality.

Tom Aiello, BASE 579, who has made more than 500 BASE jumps in the past 3 years from more than 100 different fixed objects, recently published an article on the web entitled "Getting into BASE." Under the heading "Check the fit" he writes:

> "BASE will best fit a person who is intellectually curious, has good reactions, responds quickly and correctly (without having to think during emergency), has excellent coordination and is highly organized and detail oriented. You can definitely still be a BASE jumper who has trouble with one or two of these things, but if you are weak in most of these areas, BASE is not a good sport to take up."

So far, so good, but then he gets into the BASE sales pitch, and that's were the fun starts.

> "Make absolutely certain BASE is really what you want. This sport is danger-ous, sometimes illegal and very addictive. It will take over your life. I would never advise someone to get into it (and I have found it to be the most reward-ing experience of my life). In my short time in the sport I've seen two life flight helicopters from the outside, two more from the inside, the back of a police car, several broken bones, and a funeral. I've also spent three weeks in intensive care and 18 hours in neurosurgery. Are you sure you really want to do this?"

When I read this, it took me back to our experiences, and I realized that we had been very lucky. We had been in the back of a police car, experienced broken bones and slashed leg muscles, but no helicopters or neurosurgery. Tom contin-ued with some impressive statistics:

> "There are lots of different reasons to get into BASE, and I have given up try-ing to decide which are the 'right' ones. The important thing is that your rea-sons are important enough to you that you outweigh the potentially enormous costs of BASE jumping. Unless you are a race car driver, BASE is by far the most dangerous thing you will ever do. Statistically, you have something like a 5% chance of dying by the end of your BASE career. Worse, your chance of serious injury (think hospital time) is more like 95%. I know three BASE jumpers with more than 500 jumps who have spent serious time (more than a day or two) in the hospital due to BASE accidents. Even they agree that it is just a matter of time until they are seriously injured. If you are not ready to die BASE jumping, you are not ready to BASE jump."

Personally, I know of people who have made more than 1000 BASE jumps and are still alive. But the death rate has increased in proportion to the growth in popularity of the sport. It is possible to take a first jump course (a first BASE jump course, that is) and be up and running in a couple of days. Dangerous stuff.

So what happened to my friends Scott and Bernard? Bernard is an archeologist and now spends his time digging up artifacts below Paris and Suresnes. He is married to a beautiful French real estate agent named Isabelle and they have three lovely daughters. Scott followed in his father's footsteps and became a fighter pilot in the National Guard. He spent two years training in Del Rio, Texas and then became a full-fledged pilot of the world's ugliest air craft, the A-10 War-thog. This aircraft was specially designed to fight and destroy tanks and it was successfully deployed in Operation Desert Storm in Iraq. Scott flew the A-10 for a couple of years and then he moved to Thailand where he now works as a trans-lator-facilitator-organizer for the US Airforce. Scott is the guy who makes things happen when the US special forces come to Thailand for training and fun. His 9-year-old son Robert Romeo is a born athlete and represents Thailand in skate-boarding, soccer, skiing, and climbing.

As for myself, since marrying Yolaine, I have quit BASE jumping, as I am now responsible not only for myself but for a family. Everytime my son Damien or my daughter Chloé have fun by free-climbing a 10 foot boulder or jumping from a huge rock, I tell them "Be careful. Take it easy. Don't hurt yourself". They immediately answer "If you can jump off the roof of a building, why can't we jump from a rock?". I then shut up.

The fantastic adventures Scott, Bernard, and I experienced together have made us friends for life. We keep in contact regularly and meet once or twice a year in France, the United States, or somewhere else in the world. Even though we don't jump together anymore, the feelings we have toward each other are still strong and brotherly. The near-death experiences of our BASE jumps glued us together as a strong team of sweaty, beer-drinking, adventure-seeking young men. The BASE experience helped in developing my personality in a positive way. Today, when I encounter a difficult problem, I think, "If I can jump from the Montparnasse Tower, I can figure this out, too." Simply put, I have become a mentally stronger person.

Staring Death in the eye has changed my attitude toward life. I experience severe boredom adjusting to a "normal" life of career planning, retirement insur-ance, and three weeks paid vacation. Priorities have been rearranged. Home own-ership, buying a new car, or walking around with the latest technological gadgets are way down on the list. On the other hand, on top of the list are meaningful experiences and new discoveries. The American educator Helen Keller, who was blind and deaf, expressed my outlook on life better than anybody else: "Life is either a daring adventure or nothing."

0-595-33510-1

Made in the USA
Lexington, KY
11 December 2010